THE
STEAKLOVER'S
COMPANION

presents

THE
STEAKLOVER'S
COMPANION

170
Savory Recipes from
America's Greatest Chefs

Frederick J. Simon
WITH John Harrisson AND Mark Kiffin

PHOTOGRAPHS BY Lois Ellen Frank

FOREWORD BY Mark Miller

HarperCollins*Publishers*

Recipe on page 28 © Michael Lomonaco, and reprinted by permission from *The "21" Cookbook,* published by Doubleday, 1995.

Recipe on page 162 is reprinted with permission from *Susanna Foo Chinese Cuisine: The Fabulous Flavors & Innovative Recipes of North America's Finest Chinese Cook,* published by Chapters Publishing, 1995.

We wish to acknowledge the following companies who enhanced the photography in the book by lending us samples of their merchandise:

American Home Furnishings: 1 (800) 876–4454
    Plates on pages 19 (service plate), 57, 84, 89 (salsa dish and side plate), 95, and 179
    Flatware on page 179
    Place mat on page 31
Cookworks of Santa Fe: 1 (800) 972–3357
    Plates on pages 15, 59, 69 (service plate), 109, 113, and 145
    Bowl on page 19
    Fajita pan on page 89
    Glassware on pages 101 and 145
    Flatware on page 82
    Place mat on page 152
Dansk: 1 (800) 641–8580
    Plates on pages 157 and 171 (service plate)
    Flatware on page 109
    Place mat on page 22
Dillards: 1 (800) 654–9545
    Plates on pages 31, 79, 125, 141, and 179 (service plate)
    Flatware on pages 125 and 141
Mikasa: 1 (800) 833–4681
    Plates on pages 105, 161, 171 (dinner plate), and 175
    Flatware on pages 44 and 125
    Mug on page 19 and goblet on page 171
Pfaltzgraff: 1 (800) 999–2811
    Plates on pages 22, 49, 69 (dinner plate), and 117 (small plate)
    Flatware on pages 31 and 39
Royal Doulton: 1 (800) 356–7880
    Plates on pages 35, 44, 126, 146, and 152
Villeroy and Boch: 1 (800) 575–7442
    Plates on pages 63, 101, 133, and 139
The plate on page 82 appears courtesy of Stephan Pyles.
The buffalo glyph on page 84 appears courtesy of the Eden Gallery, Santa Fe: 1 (505) 474–3319.
The tablecloth on page 126 appears courtesy of Handwork by Anne.
The pottery platter, dinner plate, and large bowl on page 157 appears courtesy of Lisa Minkin at Hecho a Mano, Santa Fe: 1 (505) 984–0933.

HarperCollins books may be purchased for educational, business, or sales promotional use. For information please write: Special Markets Department, HarperCollins Publishers, Inc., 10 East 53rd Street, New York, NY 10022.

FIRST EDITION

Designed by Joseph Rutt

Library of Congress Cataloging-in-Publication Data

Simon, Frederick J., 1937–
    The steaklover's companion : 170 savory recipes from America's greatest chefs / Frederick J. Simon with John Harrisson and Mark Kiffin. — 1st ed.
      p.   cm.
    Includes index.
    ISBN 0-06-018781-6
    1. Cookery (Beef)   I. Harrisson, John. II. Kiffin, Mark. III. Title.
TX749.5.B43S556   1997
641.6'62—dc21   96-51609

98 99 00 01 ❖/RRD 10 9 8 7 6 5 4 3

This book is dedicated to
the cattle ranchers of America
without whom this book would not be possible.

CONTENTS

ACKNOWLEDGMENTS

A few special people have made this book possible. First of all, my late mom and dad, Trudi and Lester Simon. They instilled in my brothers, Alan and Stephen, and me a love of steak and good food and an interest in the family business. Dad was my first steak-cooking instructor. I will never match his instincts for exact degree of doneness. He had no system—just the touch of a finger.

Eve, my wife and partner, has taught me so much about the subtleties of great food. My place is at the broiler or outdoor grill, and the rest of the kitchen is hers to prepare the vegetables and other side dishes. I steer clear (no pun intended). Eve believes that my love of steak is genetic.

I was fortunate to work with "the Dean of American Cookery," the late James Beard, for the last eleven years of his life. He enjoyed our products, wrote many recipes for the Omaha Steaks recipe pamphlets, and suggested a variety of new products for our catalog. I listened and never stopped learning. Because of Jim, dining became a continuing life experience for me.

Our geographic approach to steak cooking was greatly enhanced by the contributions of over twenty renowned chefs. These individuals and the restaurants they represent are among the leaders of contemporary American cuisine. Their recipes demonstrate a variety of creative possibilities that will expand our readers' enjoyment of steak dining, and we are most appreciative of their participation.

We are indebted to our consulting chef extraordinaire, Mark Kiffin. More than a fine culinarian, he has a sense for complementary foods and plate arrangements that look great. He knows no problems—only challenges. Mark's sense of excellence is uncompromising.

Through her mind's eye and the camera's, Lois Ellen Frank and her photographic team brought special interest and beauty to our recipes. She translated them into clear visual reality while retaining the desired presentations of Mark Kiffin and our celebrity chefs.

John Harrisson, our steak-loving Brit, brought his background in food, research, and writing to this book and assembled "the team." He guided us in our approach to book format, chapters, and recipes. John served as a guide, teacher, and friend to me. His knowledge of cookbook publishing kept me on track all through the process. His value cannot be measured.

I am fortunate that my son, Todd, shares the same interests and has joined the family business enterprise with intelligence, creativity, and energy. He was my partner in the formulation of our publishing goals and methods, and maintained a continuing interest in the business activities throughout the project. His insights were important.

My grateful thanks to Susan Friedland, our editor at HarperCollins, for accepting our project, making welcome suggestions about its scope, and guiding it with a sure hand.

And finally, there are many associates and friends who made themselves available to help and advise me throughout the process of producing this book. They include Jana Appleby, Wendell Forbes, Shari Gouldsmith, Dave Hershiser, Lisa Kuehl, Edward Landry, Neil Lucas, Russ Moseman, Gary Pelphrey, Marilyn Pred, Madelon Shaw, Bruce Simon, Earlene Sterba, and Curt Todd.

FOREWORD

by Mark Miller

As with many Americans, a surprising number of my early food memories involve steak. Steaks always seemed to be a designated centerpiece of special meals, and I associate them with trips I took with my mother to the meat department at the First National market (I grew up in New England). Evocative images such as the sawdust on the floor, the large butcher with the white apron, and the sound of the giant bandsaw made a great impression on me then. Occasionally, we would drive into Boston on Sundays to attend a play or concert, and we would often enjoy a meal at a steak house—Val's—where little ribbons attached to the steaks told you how they were cooked: different colors signified rare, medium-rare, medium, and well done. As I entered my teenage years, I'd sometimes go and watch soccer games on Randall's Island in New York City, and I'd look forward to being taken out by family friends afterward to eat large, thin, Mexican-style Tampiqueño steaks served with salsa and guacamole.

During my early college days at the University of California at Berkeley, steak featured in one of my formative seminal food experiences when I ate my first solo restaurant meal in San Francisco. This is an event we probably all remember. At this particular restaurant on Chestnut Street, you went to the counter and chose the cut of steak you wanted—a porterhouse, tenderloin filet, rib eye, or boneless strip—which would then be cut to order to the thickness you requested. On this occasion I selected a rib-eye filet, and then, for the very first time, I ordered my own bottle of wine. I'm not sure I was even old enough, but at least, as I recall, it was a bottle of red!

I began my professional cooking career at Chez Panisse, and it was there that I grew to appreciate the fine points of beef and great steaks. Early on, one of my responsibilities was to purchase produce, fish, and meat, and every morning I would stop by our meat purveyor in Berkeley, the C & M Meat Company, and choose the cuts we'd use at Chez Panisse.

These would then be set aside and dry-aged for us for twenty to thirty days, until the steaks' full flavor had emerged and it was time to use them. I'll never forget just how much Vince at C & M taught me in those days—how to look at the conformation and proportion between the beef's muscle tissue, fat, and bone, and how to judge good marbling. One of the more memorable steak dishes I cooked at Chez Panisse was beef filet with truffles, for a special New Year's Eve menu.

At Fourth Street Grill, my first restaurant in Berkeley, we prepared Florentine T-bone steaks, an idea I brought back with me from a trip I'd made to Italy. The steaks were rubbed with olive oil and salt, grilled, and served with sautéed spinach and garlic. I enjoyed this dish more than once during my stay in Florence, where the steaks were taken from the famous Chiana cattle, and I remember the rewarding feeling when a customer told me it was the best steak he'd ever eaten. At my second Berkeley restaurant, the Santa Fe Bar and Grill, we prepared a very popular version of Paul Prudhomme's famous blackened filet with Sauce Débris, a delicious triple-cooked sauce made with beef bones, spices, herbs, and blackened vegetables. This was one of the most intense beef dishes I'd ever tasted.

Steaks feature prominently in my travel memories. On my first trip to Japan I tried the incredibly tender and flavorful Kobe and Matsutake beef. They are so rich, almost like foie gras, that I could manage only three small slices. In South America I recall the huge grills that must have been twelve feet long and eight feet wide in the central train station of Montevideo; great beef dishes were being grilled before my eyes over a raging back fire that illuminated the whole station with its orange glow. I also visited a famous steak restaurant in Buenos Aires, renowned for the model of a huge steer in the entranceway, and I'll never forget being served an enormous sirloin steak that must have been a full three inches thick and two pounds in weight. I have a hearty appetite, and I *always* remember if I can't finish a meal—and this was one of those occasions!

Most of all, when I think of steaks, I associate them with celebratory occasions. Whether it's a birthday, the Fourth of July, New Year's Eve, or a graduation, steaks are a versatile and welcome treat. Great steak is truly memorable, and I don't think I am alone in connecting it with a time and place and a particular style of cooking. There's also something primordial and satisfying about a juicy steak, especially grilled, aged, bone-in steaks that you can pick up and gnaw on in time-honored fashion. For a chef who is interested in strong, assertive flavors, a succulent, juicy steak can carry any number of other distinctive ingredients, such as chile rubs and sauces, truffles, oysters, and wild mushrooms. Steaks provide a wonderful stage and backdrop for other foods, and they can play the leading role for spectacular results and memorable cuisine. Steaks need to be understood in terms of their unique, rich flavor, and they are an important part of the repertoire for any good cook.

Sometimes when I want to entertain guests at home, I go to my wine cellar and choose a really great bottle of red—an old, smooth Bordeaux or a "big" Rhône wine, for example, or a spectacular California Cabernet—and then I plan what would complement it best. More often than not, my choice will be a great steak to create a wonderful marriage of intense flavors. When I'm asked about the secret to a great steak meal, I reply that by far the most important element is to find a great steak. It's very simple and it may be obvious, but it's true. Soulless steak—poorly raised meat, carelessly cut and handled, overly refrigerated, and indifferently cooked—can be a great disappointment. Most of us have experienced a mushy, flavorless steak, but when you bite into a well-seasoned, perfectly cooked, great steak, there's nothing more satisfying. As I sometimes like to tell my guests, "A good steak is great, but a great steak is a thing of beauty."

Well, you are in good hands with Omaha Steaks and its association with Fred Simon, who knows a thing or two about excellence. A number of my colleagues with well-earned reputations in the field of American cuisine have contributed some mouth-watering steak recipes to this timely book that spans the regional cuisines of the United States and beyond. Steaks have no boundaries. This book comprehensively covers the art of cooking great steaks and demonstrates myriad tempting flavoring possibilities. There is something here for everyone who loves steak, and I encourage you to tend to your grill! Heat up those pans! Start up the broiler! Let's start sizzling those steaks!

INTRODUCTION
Steak in America and Around the World

by Merle Ellis ("The Butcher")

The United States has been a nation of steaklovers for a long, long time. More beef is consumed across the globe than any other meat, but per capita consumption is highest of all in this country. Steaks play a major role in this legacy, and big, juicy beefsteaks are regarded in other countries, especially Europe, as a distinctively *American* food. This steak culture has been developed in a remarkably short time, given that beef cattle are not indigenous to these shores. All domestic cattle are descended from the aurochs, the wild animals often depicted in European prehistoric cave paintings. Aurochs were worshiped and revered in ancient times, and featured prominently in Greek and Roman mythology. As cattle were traded eastward into Asia, so their sanctified status was often maintained; Indian Hindus still regard them as sacred. Aurochs were domesticated as cattle at least six thousand years ago— they were an important part of the Sumerian and Egyptian agricultural systems, for example—and they were used as draft animals as well as a source of food; wealth was often measured by ownership of cattle.

The Romans introduced cattle to large parts of Europe, and by medieval times, beef was the most common type of meat available. Historical documents show that in the 1300s sirloin was one of more than thirty different kinds of cuts of beef used in France, and it was one of the most popular. Steaks were favored by the monarchy and nobility of Europe throughout the Middle Ages, although most of the beef consumed by the mass population was salted or corned, since there was no refrigeration, and beef was not usually transported far. The Spanish raised cattle in large numbers, and it was Columbus who brought the animals, together with other livestock, such as pigs, sheep, chicken, and goats, to the New World.

By the 1580s, cattle had proliferated in their new habitat to such an extent that there was a tremendous beef glut, and at one point, carcasses were given away in Mexico City. Huge ranches were established in the rich grasslands of northern Mexico, and it was here that the cowboy (or vaquero) culture became established, along with all the accouterments—the horses, spurs, boots, and hats—that have since been identified more closely with the United States, and Texas especially. Campfire cowboy music and even the tradition of the barbecue were first developed and popularized in Mexico. It was the Spanish who brought cattle to the American Southwest from Mexico, and they likewise settled the vast lush prairies of South America—the pampas—in colonial times. As a result, Argentina has long been one of the major producers of beef in the world, and in neighboring Uruguay, too, churrasquerias, restaurants specializing in grilled beef, are immensely popular.

STEAK IN NORTH AMERICA

Even before the Spanish settled the Southwest and brought their cattle with them, John Pynchon, in the spring of 1655, drove a herd of fat cattle from Springfield, Massachusetts, to the market in Boston. That short "drive," by the way, is documented as being the first organized "trail drive" within the present boundaries of the United States. The steaks from John Pynchon's heavy steers met with instant and enthusiastic approval with Boston diners. That should not be surprising, since Pynchon was an expert in judging cattle. He had learned what it takes to make a great steak from his father, William Pynchon, who was America's first meat packer and is credited with being the first American to feed cattle in a stall. It would appear that those distinctly American prototypes that have made us a nation of steaklovers—the cowboy, the meat packer, the drover, and the cattle feeder—were all represented by the Pynchon family of colonial Massachusetts.

In 1854, *Harper's Weekly* recorded that steak was the most typical meal to be found in America. Most of the beef consumed in the East until then was raised in the Carolinas and the South, and around that time, beef from Texas began to make a significant impact on the market. That great gastronomic delight of meat lovers, a "beefsteak," that my clan (butchers) used to indulge in on Saturday nights in New York City back in the mid-1800s is described in a book by Joseph Mitchell: "The New York steak dinner, or 'beefsteak' is a form of gluttony as stylized and regional as the riverbank fish fry, the hot rock clambake, or the Texas barbecue." This tradition is believed to have started in the early 1800s when butchers from slaughterhouses on the East River would hustle choice cuts of beef sirloin from the aging room at the plant into the kitchen of one of the local saloons, grill the steaks over charcoal, and feast on them during their Saturday night sprees—washing down the beef with pints, leading to quarts, which led to gallons of beer.

While America's first butchers and cooks were having "beefsteaks" in New York, America's first cowboys—at least those who were destined to become legend—were having barbecues in Santa Maria, California. The history of the Santa Maria barbecue dates back to the early 1800s when the mainstay of the early California economy was cattle. America's first cowboys, the colorful vaqueros, held large beef barbecues at the rancheros following every cattle roundup. Over the years the tradition has been kept alive by groups and organizations in the Santa Maria Valley who have made the barbecue a specialty of all major events. Traditionalists will tell you that it cannot be done for fewer than one hundred people, but that's not true. Trust me! You can do it in your backyard.

The only secret of the Santa Maria barbecue is its simplicity—there are no special sauces or magic ingredients. It consists of thick cuts of beef seasoned with nothing but salt, pepper, and garlic salt cooked over Santa Maria red oak coals and served with toasted sweet French bread to sop up the natural juices from the serving pan. The cut of meat for an authentic Santa Maria barbecue is a three-inch-thick boneless top sirloin weighing in at 3 to 4 pounds. You sometimes find these in meat cases in this country labeled "chateaubriand." (If that is a bit more meat than you need, there is another cut of sirloin that works well, the tri-tip. Indeed, the tri-tip has, since the days of the vaqueros, become the most popular cut for family barbecues along the central coast of California. The tri-tip is a solid triangular-shaped muscle from the sirloin section that weighs only 1½ to 2 pounds, a far better size for a small family.)

While the love of steak was well established early in our history on the East Coast and in the West, it was Texas and the midwestern heartland together in the late 1800s that united us as a nation of meat eaters. It was after the Civil War ended, in 1865, that the great cattle drives out of Texas to the North began. The defeat of the South left Texas virtually bankrupt, its only wealth being the countless thousands of Longhorn cattle running wild over the Texas ranges. Returning Texas soldiers knew that the booming industrial cities of the North and East were demanding more and more beef, and forage land east of the Mississippi was becoming more scarce. And so the great trail drives that were to become American legend began. During the thirty-year period between the end of

"In 1854, Harper's Weekly recorded that steak was the most typical meal to be found in America."

the Civil War and 1895, more than ten million Longhorns were driven out of Texas over the long trails north to the stockyards and meat-packing cities such as Kansas City and Chicago. In 1871 the first refrigerated railroad car was introduced, making shipments to the East Coast much easier, quicker, and more reliable. Finally, the western range was largely enclosed by barbed wire as settlers began farming the land and staking their homesteads, and the era of the historic cattle drives was over.

In the early part of this century, the Texas Longhorn was near extinction, but other breeds were developed to satisfy the nation's craving for beef. The English breeds, as they came to be called—the Shorthorn, the Hereford, and the Angus—made their appearance in middle America, and hardy breeds such as the Santa Gertrudis, a Shorthorn and Brahman cross, were developed at the King Ranch in Texas. The stockyards of Chicago, Kansas City, Sioux City, and Omaha fed the corn of the Great Plains to the English breeds, and consumption of beef continued to surge through the 1960s. Since then, Americans have diversified and expanded the range of their diet and taken health considerations into account in cutting down on their beef consumption. However, quality has taken a front seat to quantity, and when people eat beef nowadays, they tend to seek out the best-quality, juiciest steaks they can find.

THE NATURE OF STEAK

Steaks are a nutritious food—they are high in protein and contain significant amounts of B-complex vitamins and important minerals such as iron, zinc, and phosphorous. Steaks today, like beef in general, are much leaner than they used to be, which is great news for those concerned about their health.

Aside from good genetics and lots of corn, what does it take to make a great steak? This may come as something of a surprise to some, but it takes more than tenderness to make a great steak. Yet, "Will it be tender?" is the question most people ask when they buy one. No customer has ever asked me whether a steak would have a good flavor, be juicy, or have the right texture. The universal question is always about tenderness. Actually, tenderness is only one of the several factors that play a part in our enjoyment of a good steak, and that part often is overrated. If tenderness were most important, the only steaks we would sell would be beef tenderloins. That is not the case. Many people prefer other steaks to the

"Steaks today, like beef in general, are much leaner than they used to be, which is great news for those concerned about their health."

tenderloin, not because they are more tender, but because they have more of the other factors necessary to make a good steak: flavor, juiciness, and texture.

Steaks don't come in thirty-nine flavors like ice cream, but there are differences in the flavor of steaks from different parts of the same carcass. Flavor in beef is determined by three things: the age of the animal when it is slaughtered, the "aging" of the carcass after slaughter, and the fat content. The older the steer is when turned into steaks, the more flavorful those steaks are apt to be. There is, of course, an age beyond which they would be too tough to eat, since the toughness increases with age (along with flavor). No beef animal in this country can qualify for the top USDA grades, Prime and Choice, if it is over thirty months of age, but many are slaughtered at twelve to fourteen months and lack the rich beefy flavor of a more mature animal.

Aging a beef carcass for a period of time after slaughter improves the flavor of the steaks it yields, because natural enzymes in the beef break down the fibers in the meat. A period of seven to fourteen days, and even as many as twenty-one days, of hanging in the cooler before being cut into steaks improves the flavor of rib or loin. Few markets age their beef that long anymore, but there are a few that do. If you want a steak with really great flavor, you should seek one out.

A most important contributor to the flavor of a good steak is fat. This is not the fat that you need to trim off and throw away, which is waste and should be trimmed by the butcher. The fat that makes for a flavorful steak is the marbling in the middle of the meat. Some people assume that the leaner the piece of beef, the more tender it will be; in fact, exactly the opposite is true. In the cooking process, the marbling melts and surrounds the meat's fiber cells, holding in the water-soluble proteins that are high in aroma and flavor as well as valuable nutrients. The marbling is high in aroma and flavor itself. It also adds juiciness to the meat by replacing the water that is driven off by the heat, resulting in a succulent, highly flavored steak. Steaks from the rib have more marbling and therefore more beefy flavor than those from the sirloin, which have less fat. Top loin steaks are not as tender as tenderloin, but they have more flavor because they have more marbling.

Texture is another property of a good steak often overlooked or even destroyed by a consumer concerned only with tenderness. Texture relates to density surface tension—what the experts call "mouth feel." A good steak should be tender, of course, but at the same time it should have a firmness of texture that distinguishes it from the baked potato served with it. The texture of many steaks is destroyed by the excessive or improper use of commercial tenderizers. They do their job and have their place; they can soften the bite and improve the "mouth feel" of a tough steak, but they can also turn an otherwise good steak to mush.

Juiciness in a steak, like flavor, is related to fat (marbling). It is not, as some seem to think, related to water content. A good steak will not lose all of its juice if you turn it with a fork rather than a pair of tongs, and those drippings that are lost down the drain when you thaw a frozen steak have nothing to do with the juiciness of that steak once it has been cooked.

A BUYER'S GUIDE TO STEAKS

A good steak is expensive, there's no doubt about it. The reason is that, unfortunately, not all beef is steak. The main steak area of the beef animal makes up only 20 percent of the carcass. There are only about thirty-five one-inch-thick steaks on an average side of beef. Because of the great demand for steaks, and because of the limited supply, good steaks are expensive.

The most naturally tender steaks from the beef animal come from a section right in the middle of the back called the short loin. When the short loin is cut into steaks with the bone left in, it yields three different cuts: porterhouse, T-bone, and club steaks. The porterhouse is similar to, but larger than, the T-bone. (By definition, the diameter of the tenderloin section cannot be less than 1½ inches; for the T-bone, the tenderloin can range between ½ inch and 1¼ inches in diameter.)

If the bone is removed from the short loin before it is cut into steaks, however, the selection and the terminology may become a bit confusing, and even more expensive. The boneless short loin yields, for example, New York steaks—except in New York City. They don't have New York steaks in New York City; they have Kansas City strips—which they don't have in Kansas City. They are called Texas strips there, but in Texas they're New York steak. In other places, they're called Shell steak, top loin, or strip loin. For the purpose of simplicity—and clarity—we call this cut a boneless strip here, consistent with Omaha Steaks' terminology. This cut is the top muscle of the short loin and one of the most tender muscles of all.

Rib Eye (Filet of Prime Rib)

Filet Mignon (Tenderloin Steak)

Top Sirloin

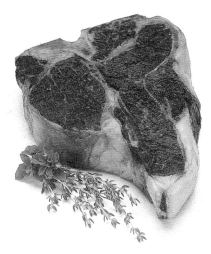

Porterhouse Steak

T-bone Steak

Boneless Strip Sirloin

It is exceeded in tenderness only by the other muscle of the short loin, the tenderloin. This is the section from which filet mignon steaks, medallions, and tournedos are cut (and the pointed end also yields tenderloin tips). Filet mignon steaks are expensive not only because of their premium quality, but also because the meat must be trimmed; nearly 1 pound of meat is required to yield a 6- to 8-ounce filet. You often can save a good deal of money on strip steaks and tenderloin steaks if you buy a bone-in porterhouse and remove the bone yourself. It contains both and usually at a better price than either.

As you move away from the short loin in either direction, the meat becomes increasingly less tender, but it's a gradual change. Behind the short loin, for example, is the sirloin section. The top sirloin comes from the thick center of the sirloin and does not contain any tenderloin. It has a pleasantly firm texture and a robust beef flavor, and because it has little marbling, it contains fewer calories. The various muscles of the sirloin are tender enough to grill or barbecue beautifully. The same is true of the rib section just in front of the short loin. Rib steaks (or filet of prime rib) and rib-eye steaks are cut from the center of the prime rib roast; both are tender, with a delicate texture and a wonderfully rich beefy flavor that is perfect for barbecue. Rib-eye steaks are sometimes called Spencer or Delmonico steaks.

Those three sections of the carcass—the short loin, sirloin, and rib sections—are what we butchers call the "middle meat" and are the source for all the tender beef steaks.

Steak Techniques and Tips

As Recommended by Omaha Steaks

STORING AND HANDLING STEAKS

Steaks, like meat of all kinds, should be refrigerated as soon as possible after purchase and kept refrigerated. Cook steaks as soon as possible after purchasing, or at least within a reasonable amount of time (preferably no more than two or three days). If using meat that has been frozen or if you choose to buy steaks that have been shipped with dry ice or a freezer pack, be sure to thaw in the refrigerator—this allows for juicier, more flavorful steaks. Never thaw meat at room temperature. Thawing vacuum-sealed steaks in cold water will speed the process; using a microwave is the least recommended method. Steaks that have been thawed but contain some ice crystals or are still cold to the touch (at or below 40 degrees) and have been held in the refrigerator for only a day or two can be refrozen. A good rule of thumb is that if a food is safe to eat, it is safe to refreeze. Seal the steaks tightly in freezer bags with as little air inside as possible, and for best results, use within three months.

To ensure the safe handling of meat, do not use the same cutting board or platter for raw meats and cooked meats. Thoroughly wash hands, utensils, cutting boards, and counter-tops that come into contact with raw food. Do not let cooked meats stand at room temperature; refrigerate leftovers immediately.

COOKING STEAKS

It is always preferable to cook steaks from a thawed state, then season to your taste. There are several common methods for cooking steaks: grilling, broiling, and sautéing (a majority of the recipes in this book call for grilling, but it is easy enough to use one of the alternative methods).

In any case, it is important to preheat the grill or broiler; for sautéing, heat the pan until it is hot before adding the steak so that the juices of the seared meat are effectively sealed in. When grilling with either a gas or charcoal grill, use a lid to make it easier to regulate the temperature over which you are cooking. Note that keeping a lid on will speed up cooking time and reduce flare-ups. Make sure the charcoals are covered with a thin layer of gray ash and have a red glow before adding the steaks.

Broiling is a high-heat method; the steaks should be at least two to three inches, and up to four or five inches, away from the heat source. When broiling with an electric oven, leave the oven door ajar. Use heavy pans or skillets when sautéing steaks, so the heat is evenly distributed across the bottom of the pan and the steaks cook evenly.

"In timing steaks as they cook, remember that bone-in cuts will take longer than bone-less steaks."

In timing steaks as they cook, remember that bone-in cuts will take longer than boneless steaks. The cooking times given in the recipes should be considered as a general guideline rather than a hard-and-fast rule. Many factors can affect timing. When grilling, for example, the exact size and heat of the fire tends to vary, and weather (especially wind, humidity, and air temperature), the openness of air vents, the height of the grill rack, and placement of the meat on the grill can all affect cooking times. Likewise, determining "medium-high heat" when sautéing on a gas stove is a rather imprecise and subjective measure, while it generally takes longer to adjust the heat using an electric stove. In addition, the exact thickness of the steaks will also affect recommended cooking times, so you need to be flexible.

When grilling, keep the rack clean with a wire brush. In most cases, lightly oiling the rack before grilling the steaks will prevent them from sticking.

The best test of doneness is to remove the steak and cut into it with a sharp knife. You may find it easier to use an instant-read meat thermometer that can be inserted into the center of the steak: for rare, the internal temperature should be 115 degrees; for medium-rare, 120 degrees; for medium, 125 to 130 degrees; and for medium-well, 135 to 140 degrees. Another means of testing steak for doneness is to touch it with your finger. Rare steak meat will feel soft and wobbly, while at medium, it will have a springy firmness. Well-done steak will feel very firm and unyielding.

In general, turn the steaks as they cook just once; they should be turned when the meat juices begin to bubble up through the meat to the top of the steak. The recipes in this book call for an even cooking time for each side, but some cooks prefer to cook the first side a little longer than the second, since the second side will be warming even while it is away from direct heat. In this case, if the recipe calls for cooking a steak for four minutes per side, you might want to cook the first side for five minutes and the second for three. Use whichever method suits your personal preference, and test the steaks for doneness as they cook.

Steaks will continue to cook a little after you remove them from the heat source, so stop cooking at the point when the steaks test slightly less done than desired.

Finally, a word about portion sizes: The recipes in this book all serve main course portions and assume steaklover-size healthy appetites. While some steak portions are for 6-ounce filets, many fall within the 8- to 10-ounce range. There are also some recipes that call for 16- to 20-ounce bone-in porterhouse steaks or T-bones. By all means choose smaller steak cuts to suit your budget and appetite. If you are particularly concerned about your diet, once again, use your judgment and adjust the recipes accordingly.

WINE NOTES

I encourage readers of this book to enjoy the experience of complementary wines to enhance the "steak experience." My wife and I enjoy liquidating our wine assets at the dining table, and red wine, to me, is an essential ingredient for a fine steak dinner. For example, there are so many great Cabernets and Merlots from California. France offers many estate-bottled Cabernets and blends from Bordeaux, as well as a wide variety of premium wines from Burgundy, the Rhône valley, and Provence. From Italy I enjoy the rich varietals that Tuscany has to offer, and I continue to be enthralled by some of the rich Cabernet/Shiraz blends from Australia that are so well balanced and harmonious with steak. Matching wine with steak is a vast subject in which I cannot claim expertise. My only advice is to enjoy and experiment. For me, finding the wine I enjoy with a great steak dinner is comparable to a successful treasure hunt.

1

The East Coast and New England

New York Strip Steaks with Mushroom-Herb Stuffed Potatoes and Boston Baked Beans

SERVES 4

For the Boston Baked Beans:
2 cups dried navy beans, picked
  through and soaked
  overnight
5 cups water
4 ounces salt pork or slab bacon,
  diced
1 onion, diced
¼ cup dark molasses
1 cup chopped canned tomatoes
1 teaspoon dry mustard powder
1 tablespoon brown sugar
Salt

For the Stuffed Potatoes:
4 large baking potatoes
Salt
Freshly ground black pepper
3 tablespoons butter
1 tablespoon minced shallot
1 teaspoon minced garlic
8 ounces wild or domestic
  mushrooms, sliced
¼ cup heavy cream
1 tablespoon minced fresh
  chives
1 teaspoon minced fresh thyme
¼ cup grated Parmesan,
  Romano, or Gruyère cheese

For the Steaks:
½ teaspoon salt
½ teaspoon freshly ground black
  pepper
½ teaspoon paprika
4 boneless strip steaks, 8 to 10
  ounces each

4 sprigs fresh thyme, for garnish

Boston baked beans enjoy a long and popular heritage: They were traditional fare for Saturday evening meals among Puritan families in Boston in colonial days. The leftovers were then eaten as an accompaniment for Boston Brown Bread on the Sabbath when cooking was not allowed. Mark Miller, author of the foreword and the recipe on page 76, tells us that the tradition of Saturday night baked beans was still very much alive in his family when he was growing up in the Boston area. One theory is that baked beans were introduced to the Pilgrims by Native Americans who cooked beans in pits, using bear fat and maple syrup. Another is that New England seafarers brought the idea for the dish back with them from Africa. Whatever their origin, baked beans make a fine side dish for the steak and potatoes in this recipe.

• •

Preheat the oven to 300 degrees.

Drain and rinse the beans and place in a saucepan. Add the water and bring to a boil. Lower the heat to a simmer and stir in the pork or bacon, onion, molasses, tomatoes, mustard, brown sugar, and salt. Transfer the mixture to a baking dish, cover with a lid, and bake in the oven for 1½ hours. Remove the lid and stir the beans, adding more water if the beans are too dry. Replace the lid and continue cooking for 1½ hours, or until the beans are tender. Remove from the oven and set aside.

Increase the oven temperature to 375 degrees.

To prepare the potatoes, cut a short, deep slit in the top of each potato. Place on a baking sheet and bake in the oven for 1 hour, or until tender. Let the potatoes cool slightly. Slice the top off each potato, cutting horizontally. Carefully scoop out the potato flesh, leaving the skin intact. Place the potato flesh in a bowl and set aside. Season the potato shells with salt and pepper.

Heat the butter in a heavy sauté pan or skillet. Add the shal-

lot and garlic, and sweat over medium heat for 1 minute. Add the mushrooms, turn up the heat to medium-high, and sauté 2 minutes longer. Stir in the cream and heat through. Remove the pan from the heat, fold in the chives and thyme, and adjust the seasoning as necessary.

Mash the potato pulp to the desired texture (smooth or lumpy) and fold the mushroom mixture into the mashed potatoes. Spoon the stuffing mixture into the potato shells and top with the cheese. Place the potatoes on a baking sheet and place in the oven to heat through and brown the cheese.

Prepare the grill. (Alternatively, the steaks may be broiled or sautéed in a heavy pan or skillet using 1 tablespoon of hot olive oil or safflower oil; they will take approximately the same time to cook as they will on the grill.)

To prepare the steaks, mix the salt, pepper, and paprika in a small bowl and coat the steaks with the mixture. Place the steaks on the hot grill and cook for 4 to 5 minutes per side for medium-rare or 5 to 6 minutes per side for medium.

Meanwhile, warm the beans through. To serve, place the steaks on one side of each warm plate and spoon the beans on the other side. Place a stuffed potato next to the beans, garnish with a sprig of thyme, and serve immediately.

Black Vinegar-Glazed Porterhouse Steaks atop a Spelt, Corn, and Green Pea Ragout

By Chef Jim Coleman, The Rittenhouse Hotel, Philadelphia, Pennsylvania

SERVES 4

For the Black Vinegar Glaze:
2⅓ cups balsamic vinegar
½ cup brown sugar
¼ cup pitted fresh cherries
2 tablespoons black currants

4 porterhouse steaks, about
    16 ounces each

For the Ragout:
1 cup spelt
1¾ cups chicken stock
2 teaspoons ground cumin
2 teaspoons ground coriander
    seeds
2 teaspoons ground fennel seeds
1 cup sliced (½ inch thick)
    smoked bacon
1 tablespoon minced shallot
3 garlic cloves, minced
1½ red bell peppers, seeded and
    diced
1 cup fresh or frozen peas
1½ cups fresh corn kernels (cut
    from 3 ears)
1 bunch scallions, sliced
½ tablespoon sugar
3 tablespoons balsamic vinegar
Salt
Freshly ground black pepper

Spelt is a wheatlike grain that was grown extensively in ancient times—it is even mentioned in the New Testament. It is higher in protein and more disease resistant than wheat, and has a higher vitamin and mineral content, which explains its recent increase in popularity. In addition, it's an ideal alternative for those who have a dietary or metabolic intolerance of wheat. As this recipe proves, spelt makes a fine ragout that also provides an interesting topic of conversation!

Balsamic vinegar is a traditional match with soft fruit (it's often served over strawberries in Italy), and this unusual fruit glaze works marvelously with the flavors of the beef.

....

Combine all the ingredients for the glaze in a saucepan and bring to a boil. Reduce the mixture by half. Remove the pan from the heat, transfer the mixture to a blender or food processor, and puree until smooth. Strain the glaze through a fine-mesh sieve into a glass dish large enough to hold the steaks. Place the porterhouse steaks in the dish, cover, and refrigerate for at least 1 hour but preferably up to 3 hours. Turn the steaks over at least once.

To prepare the ragout, combine the spelt and stock in a saucepan. Bring to a boil, lower the heat to medium, and cook until all the liquid has been absorbed and the spelt is tender, about 30 minutes. Remove from the heat and set aside.

Place the cumin, coriander, and fennel in a small, dry skillet and toast over low heat for about 1 minute, or until fragrant. Set aside.

Fry the bacon in a large, heavy sauté pan over medium-high heat until crispy. Remove the bacon from the pan with a slotted spoon and drain on paper towels. Reserve.

Return the sauté pan to the heat, add the shallot and garlic, and sauté over medium-high heat for 2 minutes. Add the bell peppers and sauté 1 minute longer. Stir in the cooked spelt, peas, and corn, and sauté the mixture for 3 minutes. Stir in the toasted cumin, coriander, and fennel. Stir in the scallions, sugar, and vinegar, and sauté for 5 minutes, until all the flavors have blended.

Prepare the grill (or, alternatively, the steaks can be broiled).

Remove the steaks from the glaze and season with salt and pepper. (Reserve the glaze to brush on the steaks immediately before serving, if you wish.) Place the steaks on the hot grill and cook for about 6 minutes per side for medium-rare or about 8 minutes per side for medium. Brush the steaks with a little of the glaze after you have removed them from the grill.

Place the steaks in the center of each serving plate, spoon the ragout around the steaks, and serve immediately.

Jim Coleman has been the executive chef at Philadelphia's prestigious Rittenhouse Hotel since 1992. He is a native of Dallas, Texas, and an alumnus of the Culinary Institute of America. Jim has cooked in restaurant kitchens around the world and has collaborated on cooking events in the United States with such leading fellow chefs as Stephan Pyles and Mark Miller. In 1996 he hosted Philadelphia's Dinner of the Decade, an event organized by the James Beard Foundation at the Rittenhouse that featured guest chefs Charlie Trotter, Emeril Lagasse, Marcel Desaulniers, Joachim Splichal, and Christopher Gross. Jim has a television cooking show, *Philadelphia Kitchens,* which airs nationally on the Nostalgia Channel, and his own radio food show, which is carried by the city's National Public Radio affiliate. Jim is also the author of a cookbook, *The Rittenhouse Cookbook,* published by Ten Speed Press.

Tenderloin Tips Braised in Samuel Adams Ale with Hot Maple Mustard and Corn Bread

SERVES 4

For the Corn Bread:
2 cups yellow cornmeal
¼ cup all-purpose flour
1 teaspoon baking soda
1 teaspoon salt
½ teaspoon freshly ground black pepper
¼ teaspoon ground cumin
1 cup buttermilk
1 teaspoon minced fresh dill
2 eggs
1 tablespoon butter

For the Hot Maple Mustard:
½ cup pure maple syrup
¾ cup prepared Dijon mustard
2 tablespoons chopped fresh dill
1 teaspoon cayenne

For the Tenderloin:
3 tablespoons olive oil
1½ pounds tenderloin tips, cut into ½-inch cubes
Salt
Freshly ground black pepper
1 onion, thinly sliced
2 garlic cloves, minced
4 Roma (plum) tomatoes, cored and diced
1 bottle (1½ cups) Samuel Adams Boston Ale

This hearty recipe has a distinctly New England flair to it, with the combination of maple syrup, corn bread, and Samuel Adams Ale, a product that Boston can be proud of. The brewery produces several types of beer, any of which would work well in this recipe, but feel free to substitute any good-quality microbrew. The darker and thicker grade B maple syrup with its full flavor is preferable to the more refined grade A; grade B has the added advantage of being less expensive. You can buy tenderloin tips prepackaged (see Resource Guide, page 190) or make your own by cubing four trimmed filets weighing 6 ounces each.

••

Preheat the oven to 350 degrees.

To prepare the corn bread, combine the cornmeal, flour, baking soda, salt, pepper, and cumin in a mixing bowl. Stir in the buttermilk, dill, and eggs, and beat gently until a smooth batter forms; do not overmix. Melt the butter in a heavy cast-iron or ovenproof skillet; there should be just enough to coat the skillet; any excess can be stirred into the batter. Pour the batter onto the skillet and bake in the oven for 25 to 30 minutes, or until the top is lightly browned.

Thoroughly mix together all the ingredients for the mustard in a mixing bowl. (If you are sensitive to the heat of chiles, add the cayenne a little at a time until you reach a tolerable heat level.) Set aside.

To prepare the tenderloin, heat the oil in a large, heavy sauté pan or skillet. Season the tenderloin slices with the salt and pepper, and add to the hot pan. Sauté the meat over medium-high heat for about 2 minutes, until the slices have browned. Add the onion and garlic, and sauté for 1 minute. Stir in the tomatoes and sauté 1 minute longer. Stir in the maple mustard and then deglaze the pan with the ale.

Bring the mixture to a boil and lower the heat to a simmer. Reduce the mixture until the liquid has thickened into a saucelike consistency, about 3 or 4 minutes. Ladle the braised tenderloin and sauce into serving bowls. Serve with the corn bread to soak up and fully enjoy the sauce.

Grilled Beef Tenderloin with Spicy Balsamic Vinaigrette

By Chef Gordon Hamersley, Hamersley's Bistro, Boston, Massachusetts

For the Spicy Balsamic Vinaigrette:
½ cup beef stock (page 186)
½ cup red wine
2 tablespoons balsamic vinegar
½ teaspoon coriander seeds
½ teaspoon fennel seeds
½ teaspoon cayenne
¾ tablespoon paprika
½ teaspoon ground cumin
½ teaspoon minced fresh thyme
¼ cup olive oil
½ teaspoon salt
½ teaspoon freshly ground black pepper
¼ teaspoon sugar

For the Beef:
1 beef tenderloin, about 2 pounds, cut into 4 equal portions
2 tablespoons vegetable oil
Salt
Freshly ground black pepper

The art of the backdoor cookout has been going through some very innovative changes in the last few years. The days of hot dogs and burgers with potato salad and beers are being challenged and maybe eclipsed by a new and creative approach toward food. Although grilling is not typical of the French bistro repertoire, it definitely plays a role in the American bistro kitchen. I really enjoy the fun of cooking outside for a crowd of people. I love the way the smoky nature of the beef blends with the warm vinaigrette. The technique for making the vinaigrette can be used equally well with poultry and fish. Serve this dish with a light, mixed green salad.

—Gordon

Gordon Hamersley began cooking while at Boston University in the early 1970s, and he trained in various French restaurants in the area. In 1979 he moved to Los Angeles and worked with Wolfgang Puck at the famed Ma Maison restaurant. After spending a sabbatical in France, Gordon returned to work with Lydia Shire at the Bostonian Hotel. In 1987 he opened Hamersley's Bistro with his wife, Fiona, on Tremont Street in Boston's South End, and in 1993 they moved the restaurant just down the street to larger premises. Gordon's creative contemporary American bistro cooking is complemented and inspired by hearty traditional French bistro fare, and he uses New England ingredients whenever he can. Gordon was nominated in five consecutive years by the James Beard Foundation for the Best Chef in the Northeast region, winning the award in 1995. The restaurant was named "Best of Boston" by *Boston* magazine for five years in a row and received its Hall of Fame Award in 1996. Gordon appeared on Julia Child's television series *Cooking with Master Chefs* and is included in the book of the same name.

To prepare the vinaigrette, combine the stock, wine, vinegar, coriander, fennel, cayenne, paprika, cumin, and thyme in a saucepan and bring to a boil over high heat. Lower the heat to medium and reduce the mixture to ½ cup. Transfer the mixture to a blender and, with the machine running, slowly add the oil in a steady stream. Blend until the mixture has emulsified. Add the salt, pepper, and sugar, and blend until just combined. If the vinaigrette is too thick, add about 1 tablespoon of warm water. Return to a clean saucepan and keep warm until ready to serve.

Prepare the grill (or, alternatively, the steaks can be broiled).

Rub the tenderloin portions with the oil, and season with salt and pepper. Place the meat on the grill and cook for about 4 to 5 minutes per side for medium-rare, depending on the thickness of the meat and the heat of the grill. Remove the meat from the grill and let rest on a platter for 2 or 3 minutes.

Spoon the warm vinaigrette in the center of each plate and spread out. Place the tenderloins on top of the vinaigrette and serve immediately.

Philadelphia Cheesesteak Sandwiches

1½ pounds top sirloin, shaved paper-thin

Salt

Freshly ground black pepper

4 tablespoons peanut oil

1 onion, thinly sliced

1 green bell pepper, seeded and thinly sliced

4 ounces fresh mushrooms, thinly sliced

4 hoagie, po'boy, or Italian-style sandwich rolls, sliced lengthwise

4 ounces provolone cheese, cut into 8 thin slices

¼ cup sliced pickled jalapeño chiles

8 pickled jalapeño chiles, for garnish

Potato chips, for garnish (optional)

Geno's, Pat's, and Jim's Steaks—three landmark eateries—are the true South Philly meccas for cheesesteak connoisseurs. If you've never had a cheesesteak, we strongly recommend putting it on your to-do list, and when you're in town, you must have the cheesesteak experience. Tell 'em Fred sent you, and make sure you have plenty of napkins at hand—this sandwich is not for the faint of heart! This meltingly good gourmet sandwich originated sometime in the 1930s, and you can tell the genuine article because the chopped shaved beef is cooked on a flattop griddle. The easiest way to shave the sirloin paper-thin is to ask your butcher to do it for you; otherwise, to simplify slicing, freeze it for an hour or so to firm it up.

• •

Season the sirloin with salt and pepper, and set aside.

Heat 2 tablespoons of the oil on a pancake-style griddle or in a heavy cast-iron skillet. Add the onion, bell pepper, and mushrooms to the hot pan, season with salt and pepper, and sauté over medium-high heat for about 3 minutes, until soft. Keep warm.

Heat the remaining 2 tablespoons of oil on the griddle or in a skillet. Add the sirloin and sauté over medium heat for about 5 minutes, turning constantly, until cooked through. Keep warm.

Toast the sandwich rolls on the griddle, remove, and place the bottom of each roll on a serving plate. Place the sautéed meat on the bottom of the roll, top with the sautéed onion mixture, and finish with the cheese slices. Sprinkle the jalapeño slices over the cheese and top with the remaining half of the roll. Cut the sandwich in half and serve with the pickled jalapeños and potato chips, if desired.

Porterhouse Steaks with Peter Luger's German-Style Hash Brown Potatoes

Hash Brown Recipe from Peter Luger Steak House, Brooklyn, New York

SERVES 4

For the Hash Brown Potatoes:

5 large Idaho potatoes
Vegetable oil
1½ cups chopped onions
½ teaspoon paprika
¼ teaspoon salt
6 tablespoons butter
Freshly ground white pepper

For the Steaks:

4 porterhouse steaks, about
    16 ounces each
Salt
Freshly ground black pepper

In this recipe we have matched a juicy porterhouse steak with the classic hash brown accompaniment from Peter Luger Steak House (a combination you will find at the restaurant). A recent *New York Times* restaurant review stated, "Getting a great steak anywhere these days is an iffy proposition, but you have a good chance of getting one at Peter Luger. Which is why the restaurant is packed, night and day, seven days a week." Food critic Ruth Reichl eloquently concluded, "Since I have only a limited number of steaks in my future, I'd like to eat them all at Peter Luger." Now that's what I call a recommendation! One word of advice: When you eat at Peter Luger's, don't order your steak well done; the waiter will claim it breaks the cook's heart!

• •

Preheat the oven to 400 degrees and prepare the grill (or, alternatively, the steaks can be broiled or sautéed in a heavy pan or skillet using 1 tablespoon of hot olive oil or safflower oil; they will take approximately the same time to cook as they will on the grill).

To prepare the hash browns, peel and slice the potatoes into ½-inch strips. Place the strips in a bowl of cold water as they are cut to prevent them from oxidizing and browning.

Drain and pat the potato strips dry. Pour the oil to a depth of ¾ inch into a large, heavy cast-iron skillet and heat until close to boiling. Divide the potatoes into 3 batches and fry each batch separately; each batch should take about 10 to 12 minutes.

Remove the potatoes with a slotted spoon or strainer and drain on paper towels. When the potatoes have cooled, cut the strips into ¼-inch dice.

Heat 2 tablespoons of oil in a clean heavy skillet. When the oil is hot and begins to sizzle, add the chopped onions, paprika, and salt. Sauté over medium-high heat for 6 or 8 minutes, or until the onions start to soften and brown.

Melt the butter in a large ovenproof pan or skillet. Add the potatoes and onions, and mix together well. Sauté over medium-high heat until browned and then season with salt and pepper. Transfer the pan to the oven and roast for 10 to 15 minutes, until crisp.

Meanwhile, to prepare the steak, season the filets with salt and pepper. Grill for about 6 minutes per side for medium-rare or about 8 minutes per side for medium. Serve the steaks with the hash brown potatoes.

Peter Luger, located in an industrial neighborhood of the Williamsburg section of Brooklyn, is a national steak house institution. It opened its doors in 1887, and the old-fashioned German beer-hall decor, with its scarred oak bar top and bare wooden dining tables, has changed little since then. Peter Luger's has been described as "the Porsche of classic steak houses," and as if to prove the point, the restaurant received recognition as the *1996 Zagat New York City Restaurant Survey* Top Steak House. In fact, it is the first steak restaurant ever in the history of the guide to receive such a high food rating (twenty-eight out of thirty). The restaurant's secret lies in its straightforward and unpretentious approach, and the tireless search for the very-best-quality meat. To this end, the Forman family, which runs Peter Luger, personally go to market almost every day and dry-age steaks on the premises.

New York Ritz Carpetbag Steaks with Artichoke, Potato, and Arugula Salad

SERVES 4

For the Vinaigrette:
1 cup olive oil
⅓ cup red wine vinegar
½ teaspoon chopped garlic
Salt
Freshly ground black pepper

For the Artichoke, Potato, and Arugula Salad:
8 baby artichokes, outer leaves
    trimmed off
1 lemon, cut in half
6 small Red Bliss, Yukon Gold,
    or White Chef's potatoes, cut
    into ¼-inch-thick slices
2 cups arugula
Salt
Freshly cracked black pepper

For the Steaks:
1 tablespoon butter
1 tablespoon minced shallots
8 freshly shucked oysters, liquor
    reserved
2 teaspoons minced fresh
    flat-leaf parsley
4 filet mignon steaks, about
    8 ounces each
¼ teaspoon salt
½ teaspoon freshly ground black
    pepper

There are several theories about the origins of this classic stuffed steak recipe. One is that it was created in the 1930s by the renowned chef Louis Diat at the New York Ritz Hotel. Another school of thought claims its provenance was much earlier and on the other side of the country—a dish that was served in San Francisco during the days of the Gold Rush in the mid-1800s. Yet another hypothesis suggests it is an Australian invention, if only because it is a very popular steak dish "down under." Whatever its origins, because of the pocket formed in the steak to hold the oyster stuffing, it is named after the type of luggage popular in the last century. This recipe is an ideal (and unusual) way to enjoy "surf 'n' turf." If you find it easier, or if it's during the summer and there's no "r" in the month (the traditional test of oyster seasonality), use canned oysters; and for a different flavor twist, grill the steaks over aromatic wood chips, such as mesquite, hickory, or pecan.

....

Combine all the vinaigrette ingredients in a blender and puree until smooth. Set aside.

To prepare the salad, rub the trimmed artichokes with the lemon halves to prevent discoloration. Combine the artichokes and potatoes in a steamer or in a steamer basket set over a saucepan of boiling water. Steam for about 8 minutes, or until fork-tender. Just before you are ready to serve, transfer the cooked vegetables to a mixing bowl and toss with half of the vinaigrette while still warm. In a separate mixing bowl, toss the arugula with the remaining half of vinaigrette. Combine and gently toss the vegetables and arugula together, and season with salt and pepper.

Preheat the broiler.

Melt the butter in a small sauté pan or skillet and sauté the shallots over medium heat for 2 minutes. Add the oysters and sauté over medium heat for about 1 minute, just until the edges begin to curl. Deglaze the pan with the reserved oyster liquor. Remove the pan from the heat and let cool. Sprinkle in the parsley.

Cut a slit in the side of the filets with a sharp knife and slice horizontally across the steak to form a pocket; be careful not to cut through the steak. Stuff 2 oysters inside each filet and divide the rest of the oyster mixture between the pockets. Season the steaks with the salt and pepper, and secure the pocket with a skewer or toothpick if necessary.

Broil the steaks for 5 to 6 minutes per side for medium-rare or about 7 minutes per side for medium. Transfer to plates, remove the skewers or toothpicks, and serve with the salad.

The "21" Club Burgers

By Chef Michael Lomonaco, The "21" Club, New York, New York

SERVES 4

2½ pounds freshly ground beef,
   equal parts top sirloin and
   top round
Olive oil
Salt
Freshly ground black pepper
1 tablespoon dried thyme
4 slices rustic Italian bread,
   ½ inch thick and 5 inches
   in diameter
2 ripe beefsteak tomatoes, cut
   into ½-inch-thick slices
1 red onion, cut into 4 slices,
   ½ inch thick

The ground beef for this recipe should be equal parts top sirloin and top round, and 80 percent lean. Michael advises: "Handle the beef as little as possible—in other words, don't knead the meat—because overhandling changes its texture, moistness, and flavor." The less compacted the burger, the juicier it will be. For the authentic "21" Club burger, you should use the peasant-style bread that Michael calls for in his recipe, but failing that, use a good-quality crusty bread and avoid the usual burger buns.

••

Prepare the grill.

Using your bare hands, shape the meat into 4 round, firm, uniform patties about 1½ inches thick. Lightly brush both sides of the burgers with oil and sprinkle with salt and pepper.

Lightly brush the grill with oil and cook the burgers over medium heat for about 7 to 8 minutes per side for medium or 9 to 10 minutes per side for well done.

Meanwhile, add the dried thyme to ¼ cup of oil. Brush the bread, tomato, and onion slices with the thyme oil and season the onion and tomato with salt and pepper. Place the bread, onion, and tomato on the grill and lightly grill both sides.

To serve, place each burger on a slice of the grilled bread and top with slices of tomato and onion.

The "21" Club, New York's landmark restaurant-saloon, was originally founded as a Greenwich Village speakeasy in 1922 and moved to its present location at 21 West 52nd Street in 1930. Over the years, regular diners have included such personalities as Ernest Hemingway, Humphrey Bogart, and Salvador Dalí. Aristotle Onassis would order nothing but the "21" Club burger and the Sauce Maison.

Michael Lomonaco, after working professionally in the theater for eight years, trained as a chef and worked in some of New York's most prestigious restaurants, including Le Cirque. He was appointed executive chef at The "21" Club in 1989 and left in 1996. He has always cooked with seasonal ingredients of the highest quality. Michael makes regular television appearances and was featured in Julia Child's series *Cooking with Master Chefs;* he is included in the cookbook of the same name. In 1995 Michael coauthored *The "21" Cookbook*, published by Doubleday.

Grilled Porterhouse Steaks with Braised Endives and Tomatoes

SERVES 4

For the Braised Endives:

8 Belgian endives
2 tablespoons butter, diced
⅛ teaspoon salt
⅛ teaspoon ground fennel seed
16 vine-ripened tomatoes
   (preferably golf-ball size)
1 bay leaf
4 sprigs fresh thyme
2 cups warm chicken stock
1 tablespoon chopped fresh
   flat-leaf parsley

For the Steaks:

4 porterhouse steaks, about
   16 ounces each
¼ teaspoon salt
¼ teaspoon lemon-black pepper

4 sprigs fresh flat-leaf parsley, for
   garnish

There's nothing like a hefty porterhouse—a bone-in cut of steak from the large end of the short loin that combines the strip sirloin and beef tenderloin—to please steak connoisseurs. For a slightly different flavor twist, we've seasoned the steaks in this recipe with lemon-black pepper, a flavored type of ground pepper commercially available in the spice section of most supermarkets. It gives meat an unusual hint of citrus and can be used with most steaks anytime the recipe calls for black pepper. The braised endives and tomatoes provide an interesting contrast of texture and flavor, with the slight bitterness of the endives mellowed by the braising process and balanced by the acidic sweetness of the tomatoes. The cream-colored, spindle-shaped Belgian endive (which is actually native to Egypt) is a member of the chicory family and is grown in darkness to blanch it and prevent it from turning green.

• •

Preheat the oven to 375 degrees and prepare the grill (or, alternatively, the steaks may be broiled or sautéed in a heavy pan or skillet using 1 tablespoon of hot olive oil or safflower oil; they will take approximately the same time to cook as they will on the grill).

Cut the endives in half and remove the cone-shaped core at the base. Rub a shallow baking dish with a little of the butter. Arrange the endives in a flat layer on the bottom of the dish and season with salt and fennel seed. Arrange the tomatoes around the endives and dot the endives with pieces of the remaining butter. Add the bay leaf and thyme, and pour the stock over the endives. Cover the baking dish, transfer to the oven, and braise for about 30 minutes, or until the endives are tender but not dry.

Turn the endives after they have cooked for about 15 minutes.

Meanwhile, season the steaks with salt and pepper. Grill for 4 to 5 minutes per side for medium-rare or 6 to 7 minutes per side for medium.

To serve, carefully remove the endives and tomatoes from the baking dish and place on one side of warm serving plates. Remove and discard the bay leaf and thyme, and reduce the braising liquid slightly over medium-high heat on top of the stove for about 5 minutes, until slightly thickened in consistency and glazed. Add the parsley to the reduced sauce. Place the steaks on the serving plates next to the endives and tomatoes, and pour the braising liquid over the steaks. Garnish with a sprig of parsley and serve immediately.

2

The
Midwest

Marinated Strip Steaks with
Horseradish Crust, Corn Fritters, and Red Currant Sauce

SERVES 4

For the Marinade:
3 tablespoons olive oil
3 garlic cloves, minced (or
pressed) to a paste
¼ teaspoon ground cumin
Dash of Worcestershire sauce

For the Steaks:
4 boneless strip steaks, about
8 to 10 ounces each

For the Red Currant Sauce:
¼ cup red currant jelly
¼ cup port wine
1 tablespoon minced shallot
½ teaspoon finely minced
orange zest
½ teaspoon finely minced lemon
zest
Juice of 1 orange
Dash of hot pepper sauce or
Tabasco sauce
Salt

For the Corn Fritters:
2 eggs, separated
2 cups fresh corn kernels (from
4 ears)
3 tablespoons minced scallions
¼ cup all-purpose flour
½ teaspoon ground cumin
½ teaspoon salt
½ cup milk
2 tablespoons melted butter

Crusting meat, poultry, and fish has become a popular style of preparation over recent years. This technique adds flavor and sometimes texture as well. In this recipe the marinade provides the steak with a flavor base that the crust elevates to a zesty peak, so your taste buds will really have a treat with this lively, succulent dish.

Corn fritters are the perfect way to enjoy the bounty of summer corn, and there's no better tender fresh corn than in the Midwest. Some of the best red currants I've ever tasted came from Michigan. The red currant sauce is an adaptation of the classic Cumberland sauce, a traditional accompaniment for beef, venison, duck, and other game, and it brings the whole dish together wonderfully well.

••

Whisk together all the marinade ingredients in a mixing bowl. Place the steaks on a platter and pour the marinade over. Make sure the steaks are thoroughly coated. Cover and let sit at room temperature for at least 1 hour.

Preheat the oven to 375 degrees.

To prepare the sauce, combine the jelly, port wine, shallot, and orange and lemon zests in a saucepan and bring to a simmer over medium-low heat. Cook the mixture for 2 minutes, until the jelly has completely dissolved. Remove the pan from the heat and stir in the orange juice and hot sauce. Season with salt and keep warm over very low heat or in a double boiler.

To prepare the corn fritters, whisk the egg yolks in a mixing bowl. Add the corn, scallions, flour, cumin, and salt, and beat until thoroughly blended. Beat in the milk and melted butter, and set aside.

Beat the egg whites in a separate mixing bowl until stiff peaks form. Fold the egg whites into the corn batter. If the mixture is too thick, stir in a little milk. Pour the batter into the molds of a non-

stick muffin tin (allow about 2 to 3 tablespoons per fritter). Bake in the oven for about 20 minutes, or until golden brown. (Alternatively, heat 1 tablespoon of vegetable oil on a griddle or nonstick skillet. Pour about 2 tablespoons of the batter onto the griddle or skillet for each fritter. Cook the fritters for about 1½ minutes on each side, until golden brown.) Keep warm.

Preheat the broiler.

To prepare the crust, combine the butter and shallots in a mixing bowl. Stir in the horseradish, parsley, and bread crumbs, and season with salt and pepper; the mixture should form a paste. Let cool slightly.

Place the steaks on the middle rack of the broiler and sear for 4 minutes on each side, until almost medium-rare (sear for 1 or 2 minutes longer for medium-done steaks). Remove the steaks and spread the crust mixture on top of each steak. Transfer to a roasting pan or baking sheet and finish in the oven for 1 or 2 minutes, until the crust browns slightly.

To serve, ladle the sauce in the center of each serving plate and place the steaks on top. Place 2 or 3 corn fritters on each plate and serve immediately.

For the Horseradish Crust:
8 tablespoons (1 stick) butter,
  softened
2 shallots, minced
2 tablespoons prepared
  horseradish
2 tablespoons minced fresh
  flat-leaf parsley
1 cup fine bread crumbs
Salt
Freshly ground white pepper

Grilled Filet Mignon Steaks with Pomegranates and Red Bell Pepper Polenta

By Chef Jimmy Schmidt, The Rattlesnake Club, Detroit, Michigan

SERVES 4

For the Red Bell Pepper Polenta:

4 large red bell peppers, roasted, seeded, and peeled (page 189)
2 cups milk
2 cups chicken stock
½ teaspoon salt
Freshly ground black pepper
2 tablespoons hot paprika
2 cups cornmeal
2 cups fresh corn kernels (from 3 or 4 ears of corn)
½ cup sliced fresh chives
4 tablespoons butter
¼ cup finely grated Parmesan cheese

For the Steaks:

4 filet mignon steaks, about 8 ounces each
Salt
Freshly ground black pepper

This recipe offers an exciting visual presentation as well as an unusual—and delicious—combination of flavors. Pomegranates, which are native to Persia and a symbol of fertility in the Middle East, are truly a miracle of nature. Their name is derived from the Latin, meaning "fruit of many seeds." The brilliantly colored ruby red seeds are separated into many compartments by a tough and bitter white pith, or membrane, which should be peeled away. This is a labor-intensive but rewarding process; the seeds are sweet yet sour, and delightfully crunchy. In this recipe they contrast perfectly with the rich, soft-textured steaks. Take care when handling pomegranate juice, as it is highly indelible. Pomegranates store well and are in peak season during the fall and early winter.

••

Preheat the oven to 400 degrees.

To prepare the polenta, place the bell peppers and ¼ cup of the milk in a food processor or blender and puree until smooth. In a large saucepan, combine the remaining milk, stock, salt, pepper, and paprika. Bring to a simmer over medium-high heat and gradually whisk in the cornmeal. Add the bell pepper puree and stir continuously with a wooden spoon for about 20 minutes, until the polenta is thick enough for the spoon to stand up in it. Add the corn, chives, and 2 tablespoons of the butter, and stir until well blended. Adjust the seasonings and pour the polenta into a parchment-lined sheet pan measuring 12 by 16 inches, and at least 1 inch high. Smooth and level the surface, cover the pan with plastic wrap, and refrigerate for at least 4 hours, until firm.

Prepare the grill (or, alternatively, the steaks can be broiled). Remove the plastic wrap and cut the polenta into desired shapes (squares, rectangles, triangles, diamonds, moons, and so on). Invert the pan to unmold and keep refrigerated until ready to cook. Heat the remaining 2 tablespoons of butter in a nonstick skillet, add the polenta, and sear over high heat for 2 minutes. Turn over and sear on the other side for 2 minutes, until lightly browned. Drain on paper towels and keep warm. Just before serving, top with the grated cheese.

Season the steaks with salt and pepper, and grill over medium-high heat for 5 to 6 minutes per side for medium-rare or about 7 minutes per side for medium.

While the steaks are cooking, prepare the sauce: Combine the stock, pomegranate juice, shallots, orange and lemon pulp, and peppercorns in a saucepan. Bring to a boil over high heat and cook for about 14 or 15 minutes, until the sauce is thick enough to coat the back of a spoon. Strain the sauce through a fine-mesh sieve into a clean saucepan. Bring the sauce to a simmer over medium-high heat and season with salt and pepper. Just before serving, whisk in the butter until completely incorporated.

To serve, place the steaks in the center of warm serving plates and spoon the sauce over and around the steaks. Garnish the steaks by sprinkling the pomegranate seeds over them and spooning a little mound of chives on top of each steak. Serve immediately.

For the Sauce:
2 cups veal stock (page 187) or beef stock (page 186)
3 cups pomegranate juice or unsweetened cranberry juice
½ cup minced shallots
1 orange, peeled, seeded, and pulped
1 lemon, peeled, seeded, and pulped
1 tablespoon black peppercorns
Salt
Freshly ground black pepper
2 tablespoons butter

For the Garnish:
½ cup cleaned pomegranate seeds
2 tablespoons finely sliced fresh chives

A native midwesterner, **Jimmy Schmidt** opened The Rattlesnake Club in Denver, Colorado, in 1985. Three years later he opened the second Rattlesnake Club in Detroit, which was named by *Esquire* magazine one of 1988's Best New Restaurants. Today, Jimmy owns several metropolitan Detroit locations: Stelline in Troy; Chianti Villa Lago in Grosse Pointe Farms; and Chianti Villa Italia in Southfield. In 1994, Jimmy opened The Rattlesnake Grill in Cherry Creek, Denver. Jimmy is a prolific author and writer, penning a weekly column for the *Detroit Free Press*. Among his books are *Cooking for All Seasons* (Macmillan) and *Heart Healthy Cooking for All Seasons* (Pocket Books), coauthored with Alice Waters and Larry Forgione. Jimmy received the James Beard Foundation Award as Best Chef of the Midwest in 1993.

Roasted Herb-Crusted Omaha Top Sirloin Steaks with Mixed Vegetables and Wild Rice

SERVES 4

For the Wild Rice:
⅔ cup wild rice
1¼ cups water
1 bay leaf
½ cup chopped pecans
2 tablespoons butter
½ white onion, minced
1 tablespoon finely chopped
    fresh flat-leaf parsley

For the Mixed Vegetables:
3 tablespoons butter
1 red onion, sliced
½ cup thinly sliced fennel bulb
6 baby carrots, cut in half
    lengthwise
1 zucchini, cut in half lengthwise
    and sliced on a diagonal
1 cup sugar snap peas, stemmed
1 red bell pepper, seeded, cut in
    half, and sliced
1 teaspoon dried thyme
¼ cup vegetable stock or water
¼ cup chopped fresh flat-leaf
    parsley
Salt
Freshly ground black pepper

The tasty herb crust in this recipe complements the steaks very nicely—mustard, herbs, and steak make a very flavorful combination. You can use the same crust recipe for other meats, including lamb and poultry, although you may want to omit the mustard. If you are a garlic lover, you can add some finely minced garlic or garlic paste to the crust ingredients.

The nutty, earthy flavor of wild rice also matches the steaks well. Wild rice is a long-grain marsh grass that is native to the northern Plains and Great Lakes region of North America, and it is still harvested from canoes in the traditional way by Native Americans of those areas, although most of the commercial growing is now undertaken on large farms in California and the Midwest. If you can obtain the traditional wild rice (which is still very much wild), don't hesitate to use it.

Here's a cooking tip for the mixed vegetables: Don't cover them while they are cooking, or the green vegetables will lose their bright color.

• •

To prepare the wild rice, rinse the rice in cold water and drain. Place the water, rice, and bay leaf in a saucepan and bring to a boil. Lower the heat and simmer, covered, for 50 minutes to 1 hour, until the water has just evaporated and the rice is cooked.

Remove from the heat and let cool slightly. Toast the pecans in a hot dry skillet over medium heat, stirring occasionally, for 5 or 6 minutes, until lightly browned. Set aside.

Heat the butter in the pan and sauté the onion for 2 minutes over medium heat. Add the cooked rice, pecans, and parsley, stir to combine thoroughly, and heat through.

While the rice is cooking, prepare the mixed vegetables. Heat the butter in a sauté pan or skillet and sauté the onion, fennel, and carrots for 3 minutes over medium heat. Add the zucchini, sugar snap peas, red bell pepper, and thyme, and sauté over medium-high heat 1 minute longer, stirring occasionally. Add the stock or water and cook until the liquid has evaporated and the vegetables are tender. Stir in the parsley, salt, and pepper, and cover to keep warm.

To prepare the herb crust, mix together the butter and mustard in a mixing bowl. Add the chives, parsley, bread crumbs, salt, and pepper, and mix into a paste.

Preheat the broiler and place the rack in the middle of the oven.

(continued)

For the Herb Crust:

3 tablespoons butter, softened
½ tablespoon Dijon or
 whole-grain mustard
1 tablespoon finely sliced fresh
 chives
1 tablespoon minced fresh
 flat-leaf parsley
¼ cup fine bread crumbs
Salt
Freshly ground black pepper

For the Steaks:

4 top sirloin steaks, about
 8 ounces each
Salt
Freshly ground black pepper
2 teaspoons olive oil

4 sprigs fresh flat-leaf parsley, for
 garnish

Season the steaks with salt and pepper. Heat the oil in a skillet and sear the steaks over high heat for 1 to 2 minutes per side. Remove the steaks and place the herb crust on one side only of each steak. Transfer to the broiler and cook crust side up for about 8 minutes for medium-rare (do not turn the steaks over). For medium, sear in the skillet for 2 to 3 minutes per side, add the herb crust, and broil for about 10 minutes. In either case, the crust should turn brown and dissolve a little.

To serve, cut each steak into 3 or 4 slices. Spoon a mound of the rice on the center of each warm serving plate and place the steak slices to the side or on top. Serve the mixed vegetables next to the steak, garnish with the parsley, and serve immediately.

Kansas City Steak Soup with Corn Pudding

For the Corn Pudding:

1 cup fresh corn (cut from
    2 ears)
4 eggs
½ tablespoon sugar
Pinch of salt
2 tablespoons all-purpose flour
1½ tablespoons butter, melted

For the Soup:

1 pound top sirloin, cut into
    cubes
Salt
Freshly ground black pepper
¼ cup peanut oil
1 white onion, diced
4 garlic cloves, minced
1 red bell pepper, seeded and
    diced
1 jalapeño chile, seeded and
    minced
½ teaspoon ground cumin
¼ teaspoon dried oregano
¼ teaspoon pure red chile
    powder
1 bay leaf
3 cups beef stock (page 186)
1 cup cooked black beans
    (page 188)
1 cup fresh corn kernels (cut
    from 2 ears)
Dash of Worcestershire sauce

This traditional midwestern beef stew probably dates back to the mid-eighteenth century and the early days when cowboys led the cattle drives that brought huge herds from Oklahoma and Texas to the stockyards and railhead of Kansas City. As an option you can add diced tomatoes to the soup, and more jalapeños or chile powder if you enjoy spicy foods. Likewise, you can serve the soup with corn bread (see page 18) instead of the pudding if you prefer.

Preheat the oven to 350 degrees.

To prepare the corn pudding, grease a soufflé dish or individual 5-ounce ramekins with butter. Sprinkle a little flour over the butter, tap out any excess, and set aside.

Place ½ cup of the corn kernels in a food processor and puree until smooth. Whisk the eggs in a mixing bowl until foamy. Whisk the sugar, salt, and flour into the eggs until thoroughly mixed. Stir in the remaining corn kernels, pureed corn, and melted butter, and pour the mixture into the prepared baking dish. Bake for 20 to 30 minutes, until the pudding has set. Remove from the oven and let cool.

To prepare the soup, season the sirloin with salt and pepper. Heat the peanut oil in a heavy-bottomed saucepan, add the meat, in batches if necessary, and sear over medium-high heat for 2 to 3 minutes, until brown on all sides. Remove the meat from the pan and keep warm.

Using the same pan, add the onion, garlic, bell pepper, and jalapeño, adding more oil if necessary, and sauté over medium heat for about 2 minutes. Add the cumin, oregano, chile powder, and bay leaf. Deglaze the pan with the stock and bring the mixture to a boil. Lower the heat to a simmer, add the black beans and corn, and cook for 2 to 3 minutes, until heated through.

When the soup has thickened, add the meat and Worcestershire sauce. Ladle the soup into warm bowls and serve with the corn pudding on the side.

Grilled Aged Rib-eyes and
Heirloom Bean Ragout with a Zinfandel Reduction

By Chefs Debbie Gold and Michael Smith, The American Restaurant, Kansas City, Missouri

SERVES 4

For the Beans:
¼ cup dried chestnut lima beans
¼ cup dried checker beans
¼ cup dried snowcap beans
¼ cup split baby chickpeas
2 quarts chicken stock
2 carrots, cut in half
1 onion, quartered
2 celery stalks, cut in half
4 sprigs fresh thyme
4 fresh or dried bay leaves

For the Zinfandel Reduction:
1 tablespoon olive oil
1 cup sliced shallots
½ cup black peppercorns
1 bottle Storybook Mountain
    Zinfandel wine or other good
    quality Zinfandel
1 sprig fresh thyme
1 fresh or dried bay leaf
3 cups veal stock (page 187) or
    beef stock (page 186)
Salt
Freshly ground black pepper

This recipe showcases not only succulent aged rib-eye steaks but also some of the heirloom beans that are grown in the Midwest. Many varieties have long been forgotten and are only now undergoing a renaissance and beginning to hit the commercial market in a big way. Use heirloom beans available in your location (health food stores and specialty stores are good sources) or substitute black-eyed peas, black beans, or lentils. The Storybook Zinfandel in this recipe is an organic wine with a well-developed fruitiness that stands up commendably to the steaks and peppery arugula.

•••

To prepare the beans, place each variety of bean in a separate stainless-steel saucepan. Add 2 cups of the stock to each pan and divide the carrots, onion, celery, thyme, and bay leaves evenly among the beans. Bring the beans to a boil, turn the heat to low, and simmer the beans for 15 to 20 minutes (the time will vary for each bean), until tender. Drain each of the beans and let cool separately.

Meanwhile, to prepare the reduction, heat the olive oil in a saucepan. Add the shallots and peppercorns, and sauté over medium heat for 5 to 8 minutes, until the shallots are caramelized. Add the wine and reduce the mixture until approximately 1 cup of syrupy liquid remains, 30 to 40 minutes. Add the thyme, bay leaf, and stock, and simmer for 30 minutes, or until about 2 cups of liquid remain. Season with salt and pepper, and keep warm over very low heat.

In the meantime, prepare the grill (or, alternatively, the steaks can be broiled).

To prepare the vinaigrette, thoroughly whisk together the thyme, peppercorns, shallots, and vinegar in a stainless-steel mixing bowl. Whisk in the olive oil until emulsified. Season with salt and pepper, and set aside.

To prepare the ragout, place the garlic cloves in a small saucepan and add just enough water to cover. Blanch the garlic by bringing the water to a boil and then draining the water. Repeat the blanching process. Heat 1 teaspoon of butter in a nonstick pan and sauté the garlic over medium heat until caramelized and golden. Set aside. Melt 1 tablespoon of the butter in a sauté pan. Add the prosciutto and sauté over medium-high heat for 1 or 2 minutes. Add the shallots, caramelized garlic, all of the reserved cooked beans, and 1½ cups of the Zinfandel reduction, and heat through. Whisk in the remaining 3 tablespoons of butter and adjust the seasonings if necessary. Cover to keep warm (or reheat when ready to serve).

Season the steaks with salt and pepper. Grill for about 4 minutes per side for medium-rare or about 5 minutes per side for medium.

To prepare the salad garnish (just before you are ready to serve), toss the arugula with just enough vinaigrette to coat. (There will be some vinaigrette left over; reserve for another use.)

To serve, spoon the bean ragout onto each serving plate. Place a rib-eye steak in the center of the ragout, arrange the arugula directly on top of the steak, and serve immediately.

For the Thyme and Cracked Black Peppercorn Vinaigrette:

½ cup fresh thyme leaves
¼ cup crushed black
    peppercorns
2 tablespoons minced shallots
¼ cup red wine vinegar
1 cup extra-virgin olive oil
Salt
Freshly ground black pepper

For the Ragout:

12 garlic cloves
4 tablespoons plus 1 teaspoon
    butter, at room temperature
¾ cup diced prosciutto
2 shallots, minced

For the Steaks:

4 aged boneless rib-eye steaks,
    about 7 ounces each
Salt
Freshly ground black pepper

For the Salad Garnish:

4 ounces (about 4 cups) arugula

Michael Smith and **Debbie Gold** are an accomplished husband-and-wife team who share the role of executive chef at The American Restaurant. Both are alumni of Charlie Trotter's in Chicago and have spent considerable time apprenticing and gaining professional experience in France. Michael was the executive chef at Gordon's in Chicago before moving to Kansas City, while Debbie worked as pastry chef at Everest and then as executive chef at Mirador in Chicago. Debbie and Michael try to break traditional culinary boundaries whenever possible, in recognition of the growing interchangeability of food styles today as people become more open to new ways of matching foods (and foods with wine). Their extensive experience with Mediterranean and boldly flavored ethnic foods largely influences their styles. The American Restaurant opened in 1974 and has received The *Wine Spectator's* Award of Excellence and the Chaine des Rotisseurs Dining and Service Award.

Broiled T-bone Steaks with Parsley Butter and a Summer Green Bean Salad

SERVES 4

For the Bean Salad:

1 pound haricots verts (thin green beans), ends trimmed
2 large ripe tomatoes, cut in half, seeded, and julienned
1 clove garlic, finely minced
3 tablespoons olive oil
Dash of red wine vinegar
1 tablespoon julienned fresh basil leaves
Salt
Freshly cracked black pepper

For the Parsley Butter:

8 tablespoons (1 stick) butter, softened
2 tablespoons freshly squeezed lemon juice
2 tablespoons chopped fresh flat-leaf parsley
Salt
Freshly ground black pepper

For the Steaks:

4 T-bone steaks, about 16 ounces each
Salt
Freshly cracked black pepper

T-bone steaks are cut from the center of the short loin and are so called because of the T-shaped bone that separates the smaller section of tenderloin from the larger top loin part. Some of my overseas friends think of T-bones as quintessentially American, and they are a popular cut among steak connoisseurs. In this recipe you can grill the T-bones rather than broil them if you prefer.

Haricots verts (literally "green beans" in French) are also known as French beans, and the technique of blanching them in boiling salted water and immediately chilling them in ice water keeps them crisp and tender while retaining all their color and flavor.

The parsley butter is a great culinary asset to keep on hand because you can also use it for fish, and it freezes well.

• •

To prepare the bean salad, bring a saucepan of salted water to a boil. Add the beans and blanch for 3 to 4 minutes. Drain and transfer immediately to a bowl of ice water until cool. Drain the beans again, pat dry, and transfer to a mixing bowl. Add the tomatoes, garlic, olive oil, vinegar, basil, salt, and pepper, and toss together. Set aside.

To prepare the parsley butter, place all the ingredients in a food processor and run until smooth. Place the butter on wax paper, form into a cylinder, and roll up, or place in a small tub and form into a large pat. Chill in the refrigerator or freeze.

Preheat the broiler.

Season the T-bones with salt and pepper, and place on a rack at least 2 to 3 inches below the heat source. Cook for 5 to 6 minutes per side for medium-rare, and about 7 minutes per side for medium, turning them once. About 1 minute before removing the steaks from the broiler, place a round or pat of the parsley butter on top of each steak and let it melt.

To serve, remove the steaks from the broiler, being careful not to let the melted butter run off the steaks. Serve with the bean salad.

Pan-Broiled Steaks with Barley Pilaf and Whiskey Sauce

By Merle Ellis, "The Butcher"

SERVES 4

For the Steaks:

4 boneless strip steaks,
   8 to 10 ounces each, or
   2 porterhouse steaks, about
   24 ounces each
1 tablespoon coarsely crushed
   black peppercorns
2 or 3 cloves garlic, minced

For the Barley Pilaf:

4 to 5 tablespoons butter
1 large onion, chopped
8 ounces mushrooms, sliced
1 cup pearl barley
2 cups beef stock (page 186)
Salt
Freshly ground black pepper

½ teaspoon kosher salt

For the Whiskey Sauce:

8 tablespoons (1 stick) butter
1 clove garlic, minced
2 tablespoons chopped onion
2 tablespoons whiskey,
   preferably Jack Daniel's
1 tablespoon Worcestershire
   sauce
½ teaspoon dry mustard powder
Dash of Tabasco sauce

Backyard barbecues are right up there with apple pie as an American icon. Now, I sure don't want to be a spoilsport, but when it comes to cooking one of today's leaner beef steaks, barbecuing, in my opinion, is not necessarily the best way. I prefer to use a cast-iron skillet, and I like to make simple sauces to accompany steaks right in the same skillet. Stir a bit of booze and a touch of imagination into whatever is left in the pan; the process is called deglazing, and it only takes a moment. A well-marbled porterhouse steak cooked this way and served with a simple tomato and onion salad is soul food for this country boy!

It was my pleasure to have dined on Omaha Steaks many times with Fred Simon and the late, great James Beard. One of Jim's favorite dishes to accompany a great steak was barley. This recipe for barley pilaf has become a favorite with my family.

—Merle

● ●

To prepare the steaks, trim off any excess fat and reserve. Press the crushed peppercorns and garlic onto both sides of the steaks and let stand at room temperature for 1 hour.

To prepare the pilaf, melt the butter in a heavy sauté pan or skillet and sauté the onion and mushrooms over medium-high heat for a few minutes, until soft. Add the pearl barley and let it brown slightly. Add the broth and check the seasonings; add salt and pepper if necessary. Bring to a boil, lower the heat, and cover the pan. Simmer for about 20 minutes. Remove the lid and continue cooking until the liquid is absorbed and the barley is tender.

While the barley pilaf is cooking, grease a large, heavy cast-iron skillet with the trimmed fat from the steaks and place over high heat. Toss in half of the kosher salt, add the steaks, and sear quickly for 2 minutes on one side. Remove the steaks and add the remaining salt to the skillet. Return the steaks and sear for 2 minutes on the second side for rare. If you like your steak more well done, lower the heat to medium and cook the steaks, turning every minute or so, to the desired doneness: about 3 minutes per side for medium-rare, 4 minutes per side for medium, 5 minutes per side for well done, and 6 minutes per side for cremated. Remove the steaks and keep warm in a low oven.

To prepare the sauce, pour off the fat from the skillet and melt the butter over low heat. Add the garlic and onion, and sauté, stirring often, for about 5 minutes, until soft. Add the whiskey, Worcestershire sauce, mustard, and Tabasco, and simmer for 1 to 2 minutes.

To serve, arrange the steaks on warm serving plates and spoon the pilaf to one side. Pour the sauce over the steaks and serve immediately.

When many people think of cooking steaks and beef, they think of **Merle Ellis**, the nation's acknowledged expert on the subject. Merle was born in Nebraska, and his career as a butcher began at age thirteen in his father's meat market in Sioux City, Iowa. For years he was a regular guest on both *The Dinah Shore Show* and *Good Morning America*. His nationally syndicated television shows, *The Butcher, Cooking Around the Country,* and *Cookin' USA,* and his nationally syndicated newspaper column have made him America's best-known butcher. Merle has also appeared as a guest on countless other TV shows. He is the author of two books, *Cutting Up in the Kitchen* and *The Great American Meat Book.* Merle now lives in Tiburon, California.

Grilled Rib-eye Steaks with
Corn on the Cob and Summer Squash Casserole

SERVES 4

For the Summer Squash Casserole:

1 tablespoon butter
3 tablespoons olive oil
2 zucchini, sliced diagonally
2 pattypan or small yellow crookneck squash, thinly sliced
1 small white onion, sliced
1 clove garlic, minced
2 ripe tomatoes, cut in half, seeded, and sliced
1 tablespoon chopped fresh basil
Salt
Freshly ground black pepper
½ cup finely grated Parmesan cheese
¼ cup fine bread crumbs

For the Steaks:

1 teaspoon salt
¼ teaspoon ground cumin
¼ teaspoon ground dried oregano
¼ teaspoon freshly ground black pepper
4 rib-eye steaks, 8 to 10 ounces each

For the Corn:

4 ears fresh sweet corn, 5 broad strips of husk reserved
¼ cup milk
Salt
1 to 2 tablespoons butter

Boneless rib-eye steaks are a favorite of mine. Cut from the very center of the prime rib, they are known for their tenderness and distinctive flavor. Rib-eye steaks are distinguished by the "flavor kernel" of marbled fat running through them. It is this marbling which softens and melts slightly during the cooking process that imparts a mellow, succulent prime rib flavor.

The squash casserole is a light and versatile summer side dish that you can pair with other main courses, and you can add red and green bell peppers, eggplant, or celery if you wish. When buying the sweet corn, look for tender young ears with small kernels; these are likely to be sweeter and less starchy than older corn. Because the sweetness of the corn turns to starch the longer it keeps, use the fresh corn you buy as soon as possible.

••

Preheat the oven to 350 degrees and prepare the grill. (Or, alternatively, the steaks may be broiled or sautéed in a heavy pan or skillet using 1 tablespoon of hot olive oil or safflower oil; they will take approximately the same time to cook as they will on the grill.)

To prepare the squash casserole, heat the butter and oil in a sauté pan or skillet and sauté the zucchini, squash, onion, and garlic for 3 minutes over medium-high heat. Add the tomatoes and cook 1 minute longer. Stir in the basil and season with salt and pepper. Remove from the heat and transfer to a shallow baking dish. Sprinkle the cheese and bread crumbs over the top and bake in the oven for about 15 minutes, until browned.

Combine the salt, cumin, oregano, and black pepper. Sprinkle over the steaks and rub in. Grill the steaks over hot coals for 4 to 5 minutes per side for medium-rare or about 6 minutes per side for medium.

While the steaks are grilling, prepare the corn. Bring a saucepan of salted water to a boil, add the corn and milk, and boil for 7 minutes. Drain the corn, season with salt, and lightly spread with butter. Tear 4 long, thin strips from 1 of the corn husks and set aside. Lay each cooked corn cob on 1 of the remaining husks, then take a long, thin strip of corn husk and tie it around the middle of the corn and around the husk on which it is resting.

To serve, place the grilled steaks and corn on warm serving plates and spoon the squash casserole next to the steaks.

Seared Filet Mignon Steaks with Maytag Blue Cheese Butter and Red Wine Sauce with Chive Potato Towers

By Chef Michael Rhoades, The Flatiron Cafe, Omaha, Nebraska

SERVES 4

For the Maytag Blue Cheese Butter:
½ cup Maytag blue cheese
8 tablespoons (1 stick) butter, at room temperature

For the Red Wine Sauce:
2 tablespoons butter
½ cup finely diced onion
20 black peppercorns
½ cup Cabernet Sauvignon wine
2 cups veal stock (page 187)

For the Chive Potato Towers:
4 large russet potatoes, peeled and quartered
¼ cup clarified butter
½ cup sliced chives
Salt
Freshly ground black pepper
4 egg roll wrappers
1 egg, lightly beaten
Vegetable oil for deep frying

For the Steaks:
2 teaspoons butter
4 filet mignon steaks, about 8 ounces each, sliced crosswise into 2 medallions
Salt and freshly ground black pepper

Steak and blue cheese are a traditional pairing—both have rich and complex flavors and complementary soft textures. Maytag cheese was developed at the University of Iowa and named after Fritz Maytag of home appliance fame, who provided the funding for the development. The Resource Guide on page 190 provides mail-order information on Maytag Dairy Farms, or you can use a good-quality imported blue cheese.

The red wine sauce provides another classic touch, but the potato towers give the dish an unexpected Asian twist. The square paper-thin egg roll wrappers (also called "lumpia" in Asian cooking) are usually sold frozen or chilled in packages of ten or twenty-five and should be allowed to thaw for two or three hours before use.

This is a hearty dish, best accompanied by the same Cabernet wine used for the sauce.

••

To prepare the blue cheese butter, whisk together the cheese and butter in a mixing bowl and refrigerate until set.

To prepare the sauce, heat the butter in a sauté pan. Add the onion and sauté over medium-high heat for about 2 to 3 minutes, until the onion turns translucent. Add the peppercorns and sauté 2 to 3 minutes longer. Add the wine and reduce the mixture until almost dry. Add the stock and reduce the liquid by half. Remove the pan from the heat, strain the sauce through a fine-mesh sieve into a clean saucepan or double boiler, and keep warm.

Preheat the oven to 300 degrees.

To prepare the potato towers, place the potato quarters in a saucepan, cover with cold water, and bring to a boil. Lower the heat and simmer the potatoes for 7 to 10 minutes, or until just cooked through. Drain the potatoes, transfer to a baking sheet, and steam dry in the oven for a few minutes (the potatoes need to be as dry as possible and have a chalky texture). Using a ricer or by hand, mash the potatoes to a fine consistency. Place the potatoes in a mixing bowl, add the butter, chives, salt, and pepper, and thoroughly mix together.

On a flat work surface lay out the egg roll wrappers with one of the ends pointing toward you. Brush the beaten egg on the 2 edges farthest away from you. Place ¾ cup to 1 cup of the potato mixture in the corner nearest you. Press the mixture into a cylindrical shape and tightly roll up the wrapper around the potato, away from you. At the halfway point, fold the corners of the wrapper in and then complete rolling, making sure there are no holes in the wrapper.

In a deep fryer or in a deep, heavy skillet with about 2 inches of vegetable oil, heat the oil to 350 degrees. Add the potato rolls and fry for 5 to 6 minutes, turning to brown evenly. Remove the rolls from the oil and drain on paper towels.

To prepare the filet mignon, heat the butter in a sauté pan or skillet. Add the steaks to the hot pan and sear over high heat for 2 to 3 minutes per side for medium-rare and 3 to 4 minutes per side for medium. The steaks should be a little crusty on the outside. Season with salt and pepper, remove from the pan, and let rest briefly.

To serve, slice the potato rolls in half on a diagonal. Stand the 2 halves of each tower with the uncut ends on the plate so that the cut end is up with the potato showing. Slightly lean 2 medallions against the towers. Place a dollop of blue cheese butter on each medallion, spoon the sauce over the butter and meat, and serve immediately.

Denver native **Michael Rhoades** grew up in a family that enjoyed cooking: His father was a chef who owned his own restaurant in Evergreen, Colorado, and both his brothers are restaurant cooks. Michael received his formal training in Dallas and worked with Stephan Pyles at Star Canyon and at other fine dining establishments in the city before bringing his culinary talents to Omaha. Michael has helped open and establish The Flatiron Cafe as one of Omaha's most exciting restaurants. Located in a downtown building dating from 1912 that was modeled after New York's famous triangular Flatiron Building, the restaurant offers a menu that features "new American cuisine," emphasizing fresh, local or regional ingredients, and innovative food combinations influenced by Michael's experience and interest in southwestern and Asian cuisines. "We like to think our steaks are the best you'll have in your life," say owners Steve and Kathleen Jamrozy.

3

The
South
and
Southeast

Hickory-Grilled Filet Mignon Steaks with
Spicy Sausage and Bourbon Sauce and Portobello Mushrooms

For the Bourbon Sauce:
1 tablespoon light olive oil
8 ounces tasso or andouille
   sausage, or smoked bacon,
   diced
2 tablespoons minced shallots
½ tablespoon minced garlic
5 tablespoons Jack Daniel's, Jim
   Beam, or other good-quality
   bourbon
1 Roma (plum) tomato, diced
1 cup veal stock (page 187)
2 tablespoons butter, diced
Dash of Worcestershire sauce
Salt
Freshly ground black pepper

**For the Steaks and
Mushrooms:**
2 tablespoons light olive oil
3 tablespoons red wine vinegar
⅛ teaspoon salt
¼ teaspoon freshly ground black
   pepper
4 filet mignon steaks, about
   8 ounces each
4 medium-sized portobello
   mushrooms, stemmed and
   black gills scraped

Hickory is a hardwood native to the southern United States; pecan, for example, is one of several types of hickory. This fragrant wood is favored for smoking meats, especially hams. Grilling meat over hickory wood or wood chips gives it a distinctive, aromatically smoky quality. Matching hickory-grilled steak with a bourbon sauce makes an interesting balance of complementary flavors, since bourbon is aged in charred oak casks, giving it woody tones. Bourbon was named after the county in the territory of Kentucky where in the 1770s a drinkable whiskey was first distilled by the Irish settlers from fermented corn.

Both tasso and andouille sausage are Cajun specialties that give the sauce additional southern authenticity. The meaty portobello mushrooms round out a satisfyingly rich and hearty dish. If it is necessary to clean the portobellos, wipe them with a damp towel but avoid washing them so that they don't get waterlogged; gently scrape the mushroom gills to remove any sand or bugs that are trapped.

• •

Prepare the grill and soak some hickory wood chips in water. (Or, alternatively, the steaks can be broiled or sautéed in a heavy pan or skillet using 1 tablespoon of hot olive oil or safflower oil; they will take approximately the same time to cook as they will on the grill.)

To prepare the sauce, heat the olive oil in a heavy sauté pan or skillet and add the sausage. Sauté over medium-high heat, stirring often, for about 3 minutes, until lightly browned. Add the shallots and garlic, and sauté 1 minute longer. Deglaze the pan with the bourbon and carefully ignite. When the alcohol has burned off, add the tomato and stock. Bring to a simmer and stir in the butter until thoroughly incorporated. Add the Worcestershire sauce, salt, and pepper, and keep warm over very low heat or in a double boiler.

Mix together the oil, vinegar, salt, and pepper in a bowl. Rub the mixture over the steaks and mushrooms. Drain the soaked wood chips and add to the coals on the grill when they are ready. Place the steaks on the grill over the coals and arrange the mushrooms to the side, next to the steaks but not over direct heat. Grill the steaks for 5 to 6 minutes per side for medium-rare or about 7 minutes per side for medium. Grill the mushrooms for about the same time, until they are golden brown and attractively marked by the grill.

To serve, place the steaks in the center of each warm serving plate. Arrange each mushroom so that it leans up against the steak. Pour the sauce over both the steaks and mushrooms, and serve immediately.

Blackened Steaks

By Chef Paul Prudhomme, K-Paul's Louisiana Kitchen, New Orleans, Louisiana

For the Steaks:

8 tablespoons (1 stick) butter
*6 filet mignon steaks, about 6 to
7 ounces each, at room
temperature*
*1 tablespoon Chef Paul
Prudhomme's Blackened
Steak Magic® or Meat Magic®*

Back in the 1980s when Cajun cuisine first burst on the national scene, Paul Prudhomme's technique of blackening—searing spice-rubbed meat or fish—caught many cooks' imagination. One of the most famous Cajun dishes of all was Paul Prudhomme's blackened redfish. Serve this dish with sautéed mixed vegetables, such as broccoli, cauliflower, or squash, and/or potatoes mashed with plenty of cream and butter and seasoned with salt and white pepper.

I'll let Chef Prudhomme tell you more about the art of blackening steak: "You can't imagine how exciting beef can taste until you bite into a blackened steak. Don't misunderstand—I have nothing against charcoal broiling, but the crust that blackening gives a steak just can't be duplicated with any other cooking method. I think it adds a whole new dimension to the taste of the meat. Blackening, like charcoal broiling, is best done outside over a hot grill—unless you own a commercial kitchen! The idea is that the spice blend highlights the natural taste of the beef rather than overpowering it, so don't overseason. Don't overcook the steaks—there's a big difference between blackening and burning! It is important that the steaks are at room temperature before you cook them."

• •

Preheat the oven to 500 degrees.

Melt the butter in a pan or skillet large enough to hold 1 steak and set it aside to cool slightly. Heat 2 large, dry, heavy cast-iron skillets over very high heat for about 10 minutes, until extremely hot.

Dip the steaks in the melted butter so that both sides are lightly and evenly coated. Transfer to a plate and sprinkle (do not

pour) ¼ teaspoon of Blackened Steak Magic® or Meat Magic® on one side of each steak.

Carefully place the steaks in one of the hot, dry skillets with the seasoned side down. (You may need to cook the steaks in 2 or more batches. If cooking in batches, clean the skillet by quickly and carefully wiping it out with a clean, dry cloth to avoid leaving a burned taste.) Sprinkle with the remaining seasoning and cook the steaks for about 2 minutes on the first side and about 1½ minutes on the second.

Transfer the steaks to the second hot, dry skillet and finish in the oven for 3 to 4 minutes for medium-rare, turning once. (For medium, cook slightly longer in the skillet and 1 or 2 minutes longer in the oven.) Serve with mashed potatoes and mixed vegetables if desired.

From an inauspicious storefront location in New Orleans's famous French Quarter, **Chef Paul Prudhomme** has propelled the distinctive cuisine of his native Louisiana into the international spotlight and left an indelible stamp on the culinary world. Born and raised in Louisiana's Arcadiana countryside, Paul began cooking as a child alongside his mother, whom he proudly credits as his greatest influence. He opened K-Paul's Louisiana Kitchen in July 1979 and before long became one of America's best-known chefs, making many guest appearances on major television network programs. He has worked tirelessly to help raise funds for several charitable causes and has filmed several television cooking series. Paul is also a prolific best-selling author; among his extremely popular and diverse cookbooks are *Chef Paul Prudhomme's Louisiana Kitchen, The Prudhomme Family Cookbook, Fork in the Road,* and *Fiery Foods That I Love.*

Beef Medallions with Wilted Collard Greens and Tobacco Onion Rings

SERVES 4

For the Onion Rings:
1 cup all-purpose flour
½ cup cornstarch
½ teaspoon ground cumin
2 teaspoons pure red chile
    powder
¼ teaspoon salt
Vegetable oil
3 onions, thinly sliced, rings
    separated

For the Collard Greens:
4 ounces smoked bacon slices,
    cut into 1-inch-wide strips
2 shallots, minced
2 garlic cloves, minced
1½ pounds collard greens,
    stemmed and thoroughly
    rinsed
1 teaspoon Tabasco sauce,
    Coyote Cocina Howlin' Hot
    Sauce, or Habanero Sauce
    (page 68)
¼ cup vegetable or chicken stock
Salt

For the Beef Medallions:
¼ teaspoon salt
¼ teaspoon ground fennel seed
½ teaspoon freshly cracked
    black pepper
4 filet mignon steaks, about
    8 ounces each, cut in half
    horizontally into medallions
Worcestershire sauce
1 tablespoon light olive oil
1 tablespoon butter

Collard greens are typically southern and are grown in the region almost exclusively, although they are a variety of cabbage native to Africa (they are still featured in a national dish of Ethiopia). Collards were brought over during the days of the slave trade, and to further confuse their identity, their name is derived from an Anglo-Saxon word, "colewort," meaning cabbage plant. This recipe follows the traditional southern style of cooking collard greens—with bacon—and their chewy texture suits the smooth steak medallions very well. For best results, leave the collard greens damp after washing them so they steam nicely in the pan and do not dry out.

Why "tobacco" onion rings? Because of the toasty, smoky aroma that fills the air when they're fried. The spicy flour and cornstarch coating will help keep the onion rings crisp even though you need to make them a little ahead of time.

....

To prepare the onion rings, thoroughly mix together the flour, cornstarch, cumin, chile powder, and salt in a large mixing bowl. Heat the oil in a deep fryer or saucepan to 350 degrees. Toss the onions in the dry mixture and gently shake off any excess. Cooking in batches and using tongs, carefully place the coated onions in the hot oil and fry until crispy and golden brown. Remove the onions with a slotted spoon and drain on paper towels. Keep warm.

To prepare the collard greens, heat a sauté pan, add the bacon, and sauté over medium heat until almost crisp. Add the shallots and garlic, and sauté for 1 minute. Add the damp collard greens and sauté over medium-high heat for 2 to 3 minutes, until wilted. Add the hot sauce and stock, and cook until almost all the liquid has evaporated. Season lightly with salt, cover, and keep warm over very low heat.

To prepare the medallions, mix together the salt, fennel seed, and pepper in a small bowl. Lightly coat both sides of the medallions with the seasoning mix and then add a dash of Worcestershire sauce. Heat the oil and butter in a heavy-bottomed skillet or sauté pan until almost smoking. Add the medallions and sear the meat for about 2 to 3 minutes on each side for medium-rare and 4 to 5 minutes per side for medium.

To serve, place a mound of the greens on one side of each warm serving plate and lean 2 medallions against the greens. Place the onion rings on top of the medallions and serve immediately.

Pecan Cold-Smoked Strip Steaks with Carolina BBQ Sauce and Green Tomato Grits

By Chef Kevin Rathbun, Nava, Atlanta, Georgia

SERVES 6

For the Marinade and BBQ Sauce:

1½ cups water
1⅓ cups apple cider vinegar
6 tablespoons brown sugar
⅔ cup tomato ketchup
1 tablespoon dried red pepper
flakes
2 teaspoons minced garlic
1 teaspoon dried sassafras
2 tablespoons bourbon
1 tablespoon sugar
1 tablespoon salt
2 teaspoons freshly cracked
black pepper

For the Steaks:

6 boneless strip steaks,
10 to 12 ounces each

For the Green Tomato Grits:

5 green tomatoes, sliced
2 cups heavy cream
2 garlic cloves
1 wild onion or scallion,
chopped
1 cup medium-ground hominy
grits or polenta
Salt
Freshly ground black pepper

This delicious southern-style recipe calls for the steaks to be smoked, and if you don't own a home smoker, consider this a call to culinary arms. You can buy a small, good-quality smoker for less than $100 in camping stores or specialty kitchen stores, and they are well worth the investment. Or you may prefer to grill the steaks over pecan wood chips using low heat. The steaks should be marinated for ten to twelve hours, so begin the process early in the day. The marinade serves a double purpose, since it's boiled to make a tangy barbecue sauce. For notes on wild onions, also called ramps or wild leeks, see page 102. Sassafras, one of the ingredients in the marinade, is the herb derived from tree bark used for flavoring root beer. It's also one of the components of filé powder, an essential seasoning in Creole cooking.

••

Thoroughly mix together all the marinade ingredients in a large shallow dish or bowl. Add the steaks and turn to cover with the marinade. Cover the dish and refrigerate for 10 to 12 hours, turning every 2 hours or so to marinate evenly.

Prepare the smoker by building a small fire with charcoal and an electric starter element. Soak some pecan shells and/or pecan wood chips in water. Fill the water tray of the smoker with ice cubes, and when the coals are a uniform gray color (after about 30 minutes), place the soaked pecan shells or chips on the coals. Set the grill rack at its highest position and add the marinated steaks (reserving the marinade). Cover the smoker, sealing all but one small vent. Replenish the charcoal and soaked pecan shells or wood chips as necessary and continue to smoke the steaks for 2 to 3 hours, keeping the temperature at around 90 to 100 degrees.

Prepare the grill (or, alternatively, the steaks can be broiled). If grilling, soak some hickory wood chips in water and add to the charcoal just before you are ready to grill.

To prepare the grits, grill the tomato slices over the hickory wood chips. Transfer the grilled tomatoes to a blender, add the cream, garlic, and wild onion, and puree until smooth. Transfer the mixture to a heavy saucepan and bring to a boil. Add the grits and, stirring constantly, cook the mixture for 18 to 20 minutes. Season with salt and pepper and keep warm.

Meanwhile, add some soaked pecan shells or wood chips to the grill. Remove the steaks from the smoker and finish on the grill to the desired doneness.

Place the marinade in a saucepan and bring to boil, stirring occasionally. To serve, place the steaks on warm serving plates and pour the barbecue sauce over. Serve with the grits.

Kevin Rathbun is the executive chef and partner at Nava, an Atlanta restaurant that serves foods with Latin and Native American influences, and features ingredients indigenous to the South and Southwest. Kevin was born and raised in Kansas City, where he apprenticed with Bradley Ogden at The American Restaurant. He then worked with the Brennan family at Brennan's in Houston and Commander's Palace in New Orleans before becoming the executive chef of the acclaimed Baby Routh, Stephan Pyles's Dallas restaurant. Kevin was voted one of the country's top five rising chef superstars for 1993–94 by the James Beard Foundation, and his recipes have been featured in several nationally published cookbooks and food magazines, including *Bon Appétit* and *Food & Wine*.

Panfried Sirloin Steaks with Succotash and Barbecued Corn Sauce

For the Barbecued Corn Sauce:
1 tablespoon butter
2 tablespoons light olive oil
1 tablespoon minced garlic
2 scallions, thinly sliced
½ red bell pepper, seeded and minced
¾ cup fresh corn kernels (cut from 1 large ear)
2 Roma (plum) tomatoes, cored, seeded, and finely diced
½ tablespoon barbecue spice seasoning
2 cups veal stock (page 187) or beef stock (page 186)
Salt
Freshly ground black pepper
1 tablespoon minced fresh cilantro

Succotash is a popular dish in the South and is identified with that region, but the name is derived from the Narraganset Indian word "misickquatash," meaning corn stew. Other Native American groups in the southern and eastern regions of the continent used similar words to describe versions of the same dish. The pleasingly complex flavor of the barbecued corn sauce complements the panfried steak beautifully and brings the whole dish together. This recipe makes a great summer dish, and if you prefer to grill the steak and make an outdoor meal of it, go right ahead.

....

To prepare the sauce, heat the butter and oil in a heavy sauté pan or skillet. Add the garlic, scallions, bell pepper, and corn, and sauté over medium heat for 2 minutes. Add the tomatoes, barbecue seasoning, and stock, and bring the mixture to a boil over medium-high heat. Lower the heat slightly and simmer for 5 minutes, or until the sauce is thick enough to coat the vegetables. Season with salt and pepper, and stir in the cilantro. Keep warm over very low heat or in a double boiler.

To prepare the succotash, melt the butter in a heavy sauté pan or skillet. Add the corn and beans, and sauté over medium-high heat for 1 minute. Add the stock and simmer for about 5 minutes, or until the pan is almost dry. Stir in the salt, pepper, paprika, parsley, and Tabasco. Cover the pan and keep warm over very low heat.

Season the steaks on both sides with the salt, pepper, and ground fennel. Heat the oil and butter in a heavy sauté pan or skillet. Add the steaks to the hot pan and cook over medium-high heat for 5 to 6 minutes per side for medium-rare or 7 to 8 minutes per side for medium, turning the steaks a couple of times as they cook.

For the Succotash:
2 tablespoons butter
1 cup fresh corn kernels (cut
    from 2 small ears)
1 cup shelled fresh lima beans
    or finely shredded green
    beans
¼ cup vegetable stock or water
Salt
Freshly ground black pepper
⅛ teaspoon paprika
1 tablespoon chopped fresh
    flat-leaf parsley
Dash of Tabasco
    sauce(optional)

For the Steaks:
4 top sirloin steaks, about
    10 ounces each
Salt
Freshly ground black pepper
Pinch of ground fennel seed
2 tablespoons olive oil
1 tablespoon butter

To serve, ladle the corn sauce onto warm serving plates. Place the steaks in the center of the plates and top with a tablespoon of the succotash. Spoon the remaining succotash on the side and serve immediately.

Thyme and Fennel-Rubbed Strip Steaks with Pickled Okra and Creamy Coleslaw

SERVES 4

For the Pickled Okra:
1½ cups white vinegar
1 cup water
2 small red tabasco, fiesta, or
    serrano chiles
4 garlic cloves
½ tablespoon mustard seeds
2 tablespoons black peppercorns
1 tablespoon salt
1 pound okra, washed
    thoroughly and stems
    trimmed

For the Coleslaw:
1 small head green cabbage,
    cored and shredded
1 small carrot, grated
2 small scallions, finely sliced
¾ cup prepared mayonnaise
3 tablespoons vegetable oil
¼ cup sour cream
1 teaspoon caraway seeds
2 dashes Tabasco sauce
    (optional)
Salt
Freshly ground black pepper

For the Steaks:
¼ teaspoon ground fennel seed
¼ teaspoon ground dried thyme
¼ teaspoon salt
¼ teaspoon freshly ground black
    pepper
4 boneless strip steaks, about
    9 ounces each

This is a fine summer dish, and the herb-rubbed steaks taste even better eaten outdoors with the refreshing accompaniments. Okra, like collards, was brought from its native Ethiopia to the South by slaves, and it is a primary ingredient in gumbo. Don't let the fact that the pickled okra needs two or three weeks to marinate deter you from making this recipe. Although homemade pickles always taste best, there are some perfectly acceptable commercial products on the market that you can use if you haven't planned ahead. Make the pickles anyway, and make them regularly—you'll find yourself using them with all kinds of foods. Use this coleslaw recipe for picnics, barbecues, and cookouts, and impress your company by letting them know that the word "coleslaw" is derived from a Dutch word, "koolsla," meaning cool cabbage, which certainly seems appropriate.

•••

To prepare the okra, sterilize in boiling water 2 pint-size glass bottling jars with matching lids and rubber rings.

Meanwhile, place the vinegar, water, chiles, garlic, mustard seeds, peppercorns, and salt in a saucepan and bring to a boil. Add the okra, return to a boil, and remove from the heat. Take the hot glass jars out of the boiling water with tongs and invert to drain any water. Using the tongs, transfer the okra from the saucepan to the jars, alternating the thicker stem ends and the thin ends. Evenly divide the chiles, garlic, mustard seeds, and peppercorns among the jars. Fill the jars to within ¼ inch of the top with the liquid and seal the jars quickly, securing with the rubber ring and lid. Store in a cool dark place for at least 2 to 3 weeks before using.

To prepare the coleslaw, mix the cabbage, carrot, and scallions in a mixing bowl. In a separate bowl, mix together the mayonnaise, oil, sour cream, caraway seeds, Tabasco, salt, and pepper. Pour the mayonnaise mixture into the cabbage mixture and thoroughly combine. Refrigerate for at least 2 hours for the flavors to marry. Bring to room temperature before serving.

Preheat the broiler.

Mix together the fennel, thyme, salt, and pepper in a bowl. Rub the steaks with the mixture. Place the steaks under the broiler, about 2 or 3 inches away from the heat source, and broil for 4 to 5 minutes per side for medium-rare or 6 to 7 minutes for medium.

To serve, place the steaks on room-temperature serving plates and spoon the coleslaw next to the steaks. Arrange 4 or 5 pickled okra spears on each plate and serve immediately.

Seared and Roasted Filet Mignon Steaks with a Porto Reduction, Crumbled Cabrales Cheese, Spanish Brandied Currants, & Sizzled Leeks

By Chef Norman Van Aken, Norman's, Coral Gables, Florida

SERVES 4

For the Spanish Brandied Currants:
¼ cup dried currants
½ cup Spanish brandy (such as Cardenal Mendoza)

For the Steak:
4 filet mignon steaks,
    7 to 8 ounces each
1 tablespoon virgin olive oil
1 tablespoon freshly cracked
    black pepper
2 tablespoons fresh sage leaves,
    roughly chopped

For the Porto Reduction:
¼ cup black peppercorns
1 cup port wine
2 cups veal stock (page 187)

For the Leeks:
Peanut or vegetable oil
2 leeks, finely julienned
Salt and freshly cracked black
    pepper to taste

1 tablespoon safflower or peanut
    oil
4 ounces Cabrales cheese,
    crumbled

The New World was discovered by the Spanish (although Columbus himself was from Genoa, Italy), and the influence of Spain continues to be felt in the cultural identity of cities such as Miami. It is appropriate, then, that Norman Van Aken brings a Spanish theme to this recipe. Cabrales is a pungent blue cheese from the mountains of the Asturias region of northern Spain, and although cow's milk is the main ingredient, sheep milk and goat milk are sometimes added. Traditionally, the crusty cheese is distinctively wrapped in sycamore leaves. You can substitute Italian Gorgonzola or a good-quality domestic blue cheese. The reduced port sauce and Spanish brandy give this dish a further Iberian twist. Norman explains that he leaves the whole peppercorns in the Porto reduction deliberately, so that after extensive simmering they become almost as soft as green peppercorns and contrast nicely with the sweetness of the currants; however, you may strain them if you prefer.

• •

To prepare the brandied currants, combine the currants and brandy in a bowl, cover, and let soak at room temperature for a minimum of 1 hour and up to 3 days.

To prepare the steaks, rub the filets with the oil and coat with the black pepper and sage. Place on a plate, cover, and keep refrigerated.

To prepare the Porto reduction, toast the peppercorns in a dry, small, heavy saucepan over medium heat, stirring frequently, for 1 or 2 minutes, until fragrant and they begin to smoke. Add the port and cook over medium-high heat for about 5 minutes, or until the port is reduced by half. Add the stock and reduce the mixture for about 30 minutes, or until ½ cup of liquid remains. Remove from the heat and reserve.

Meanwhile, to prepare the leeks, heat the oil in a deep fryer or large, heavy saucepan to 375 degrees. Deep-fry the leeks in large-handful batches, stirring quickly with tongs to keep them separated as they cook. Deep-fry for 2 to 3 minutes, until golden and crisp. Remove from the oil with a slotted spoon and drain on paper towels. Season with salt and pepper, and keep warm in a low oven until ready to serve.

To cook the steaks, place a large sauté pan over high heat until very hot. Add the oil and carefully place the steaks in the hot pan. Shake the pan immediately so the steaks do not stick to the pan. Sear for about 4 minutes per side for rare, 5 to 6 minutes per side for medium-rare, or about 7 minutes per side for medium, until crisp and slightly charred on the outside, shaking the pan occasionally. Remove the filets from the pan and set aside on a warm plate.

With the hot pan removed from the heat, strain the brandy from the currants into it. Carefully return the pan to the heat and deglaze over medium-high heat. Let the alcohol burn off and cook until the brandy is reduced by half. Add the reserved Porto reduction and reduce the mixture until thick enough to coat the back of a spoon. Stir in the rehydrated currants.

To serve, drizzle the sauce around the outer rim of each serving plate. Crumble the Cabrales cheese over the sauce. Slice the steaks, lay them in the center of each plate, arrange the sizzled leeks on top of the steaks, and serve immediately.

Norman Van Aken is the chef and co-owner of the award-winning restaurant Norman's in the historic Coral Gables section of Miami. Norman was first acknowledged as the originator of South Florida's vibrant "New World Cuisine" while he was cooking in Key West in the 1980s. Norman is self-taught and was recently awarded an honorary doctorate by Johnson & Wales University, one of the premier culinary schools in America. Norman and his restaurant have received many honors, including nomination as the James Beard Foundation's Best New Restaurant in America, 1995, and *Bon Appétit*'s accolade as One of the Best New Restaurants in the Country, 1995. He also received the 1996 Robert Mondavi Culinary Award of Excellence. Norman wrote the first cookbook on the new Florida cooking, *Feast of Sunlight*, and is the author of *The Great Exotic Fruit Book* (Ten Speed Press). His latest cookbook, *Norman Van Aken's New World Cuisine*, will be published by Random House in 1997.

Jerked Rib-eye Steaks with Yuca Chips and Habanero Sauce

SERVES 4

For the Steaks:
4 rib-eye steaks, about 10 ounces each
2 tablespoons light olive oil
1 tablespoon Jamaican jerk spice seasoning

For the Habanero Sauce:
½ cup minced carrot
2 tablespoons minced white onion
2 cloves garlic, minced
2 orange habanero chiles, seeded and minced
½ cup sugar
1 cup unseasoned rice vinegar
Pinch of salt

For the Yuca Chips:
1½ pounds yuca
4 cups vegetable oil or light peanut oil
Salt
1 lime, cut into wedges

R ib-eye steaks cut from the loin end, rather than the chuck end, are much leaner and are preferred for this recipe. The steaks are rubbed with ready-made jerk seasoning, which is a typical and traditional Jamaican preparation for meat that was originally used as a practical means of preserving it. The "jerking" technique has crossed the Caribbean and is now featured on the menus of many Florida restaurants, fitting well into the region's exciting hybrid style of cooking.

Yuca (also known as cassava and manioc) is a staple root vegetable of the Caribbean that has a white flesh and makes great fries. Sweet potato fries (page 176) or regular potato fries make very acceptable substitutes.

The sauce in this recipe features the habanero, the hottest chile of all, so be warned! When handling hot chiles, it's best to use rubber gloves, and always wash your hands thoroughly afterward because the oils are very pervasive. Most important, never rub your eyes while working with chiles.

．．

To prepare the steaks, rub them with oil and season with jerk spice. (Sprinkle the steaks with a little salt if the jerk spice does not contain any.) Place the seasoned steaks on a platter, cover with plastic wrap, and let sit at room temperature for 1 hour.

Meanwhile, to prepare the sauce, place all the ingredients in a saucepan with 1 cup of water and bring to a boil. Boil over medium-high heat for about 15 minutes, or until the liquid is reduced by half. Transfer to a blender and puree. Set aside and let cool.

Prepare the grill (or, alternatively, the steaks may be broiled or sautéed in a heavy pan or skillet, using 1 tablespoon of hot olive oil or safflower oil; they will take approximately the same time to cook as they will on the grill).

To prepare the chips, bring a saucepan of water to a boil. Peel the yuca with a large, heavy knife and cut into paper-thin slices (preferably with a mandolin slicer). In a deep fryer or large, heavy skillet, heat the oil to 375 degrees. Carefully add the yuca slices in batches and fry for about 20 to 30 seconds, until crispy and golden brown. Remove the chips with a slotted spoon and drain on paper towels. Immediately season with salt and sprinkle with lime juice squeezed from the wedges. Keep warm in a low oven.

Place the seasoned steaks on the hot grill and cook for 4 to 5 minutes per side for medium-rare or 6 to 7 minutes per side for medium.

To serve, place each steak on the side of a warm serving plate and top with the sauce. Place the chips next to the steak and serve immediately.

Skirt Steak with Red Wine Mojo and Orange Salsa

By Chef Allen Susser, Chef Allen's, Aventura, Florida

SERVES 4

For the Red Wine Mojo:
1 cup dry red wine
¼ cup honey
1 tablespoon minced ginger
1 tablespoon minced garlic
½ cup freshly squeezed orange
   juice
¼ cup freshly squeezed lime
   juice
½ teaspoon kosher salt
½ teaspoon freshly ground black
   pepper

For the Steak:
2 pounds skirt steak
½ teaspoon kosher salt
½ teaspoon freshly ground black
   pepper

For the Orange Salsa:
2 large Roma (plum) tomatoes
2 large oranges, peeled,
   sectioned, and diced
1 large sweet onion, finely diced
2 large jalapeño chiles, seeded
   and minced
2 tablespoons freshly squeezed
   lime juice
½ cup freshly squeezed orange
   juice
2 tablespoons chopped fresh
   cilantro
½ teaspoon kosher salt

4 sprigs fresh cilantro, for
   garnish

Skirt steak is a flavorful cut, most commonly used for southwestern fajitas, but it tends to be a little tougher than filet or sirloin steak, so marinating helps tenderize it. If you prefer, you can use strip steak instead.

This recipe reflects the light, fruity, and tropical tones of contemporary Florida cuisine, and the mojo (pronounced "mo-ho") gives it a Caribbean touch. A mojo is a marinade or salsa typical of Cuban cuisine, and it is used here as the former. By definition, a mojo always contains citrus juice, garlic, and some type of herb.

· ·

To prepare the mojo, place the wine in a saucepan and bring to a simmer. Remove the pan from the heat and stir in the honey, ginger, and garlic. Let the mixture sit for 10 minutes, then stir in the orange juice, lime juice, salt, and pepper. Set aside to cool completely.

Place the steak in a large, shallow dish, season with salt and pepper, and pour the mojo over it. Cover with plastic wrap and refrigerate for 1 hour.

To prepare the salsa, bring a small saucepan of water to a boil and blanch the tomatoes for 30 seconds. Remove the tomatoes and plunge into cold water. Peel with the tip of a knife, then gently squeeze out the seeds and dice the tomato. Transfer to a mixing bowl, add the remaining salsa ingredients, and mix together thoroughly. Let the salsa stand at room temperature for 30 minutes before serving to allow the flavors to marry.

Prepare the grill (or, alternatively, the steaks can be broiled). Remove the steak from the mojo and wipe off any excess. Place the meat on the hot grill and cook for about 2 to 3 minutes per side for medium-rare or 3 to 4 minutes per side for medium. Remove the steak from the grill, transfer to a platter, and let it sit for 3 minutes before slicing.

To serve, slice the steak on a diagonal, against the grain. Arrange the slices on a serving platter and garnish with the cilantro. Serve with the orange salsa on the side.

> Resolving at an early age to pursue a career in the culinary arts, Brooklyn-born **Allen Susser** trained in New York and Florida, and gained professional experience in the kitchens of the prestigious Bristol Hotel in Paris and Le Cirque restaurant in New York. Working next at the Turnberry Isle Resort in Florida, Allen began synthesizing the foods of his adopted region, steadily incorporating influences from the Caribbean, Latin America, and modern American cuisine. In 1986 Allen opened his own restaurant, Chef Allen's, in Aventura. Allen was named Best New Chef in America in 1991 by *Food & Wine* magazine, and in 1994 he received the James Beard Foundation's Best Chef Award for the southeast region. In 1995 he was awarded an honorary doctorate from Johnson & Wales University. His first cookbook, *New World Cuisine and Cookery,* was published by Doubleday in 1995.

4

The Western Range and the Great Southwest

Red Chile Filets with Smoky Barbecue Sauce and Spicy Mashed Potatoes

For the Red Chile Rub:
¼ cup dried red pepper flakes
½ tablespoon dried oregano
¼ cup pure red chile powder
1 teaspoon sugar
½ teaspoon salt

For the Steaks:
4 filet mignon steaks, about 7 to
  8 ounces each

For the Smoky Barbecue Sauce:
1 teaspoon allspice berries
2 teaspoons cloves
1½ tablespoons coriander seeds
1 cup cider vinegar
3 tablespoons olive oil
4 cloves garlic, minced
½ onion, minced
⅓ cup brown sugar
3 tablespoons dark molasses
1 teaspoon Worcestershire sauce
¾ cup Negra Modelo or other
  dark beer
¼ cup puréed canned chipotle
  chiles in adobo sauce
1¼ cups tomato ketchup

Spice rubs, such as the red chile mixture used for the filets in this recipe, are a technique for marinating steaks using dry ingredients, which is why the steaks are left to sit for thirty minutes to absorb the flavors of the rub. If you want the flavors accentuated—and, in this case, the heat of the chile to thoroughly permeate the steaks—you can let the filets marinate longer, refrigerated. Just remember to bring them to room temperature before grilling or the interior of the meat will be undercooked relative to the outside.

The spice rub pairs with the barbecue sauce very well, and you can use the sauce with other meats, including brisket and burgers. If you want to enhance or vary the flavor of the mashed potatoes, add a tablespoon of finely sliced fresh chives or minced cilantro, or substitute ¼ cup of sour cream for an equal amount of milk.

• •

To prepare the red chile rub, combine the red pepper flakes and oregano in a dry skillet and toast over medium heat for 2 minutes, until fragrant. Transfer to a spice grinder and pulse until finely ground. Place in a bowl, add the red chile powder, sugar, and salt, and mix together thoroughly.

Massage the red chile rub into the filets. Place the steaks on a platter, cover with plastic wrap, and let sit at room temperature for 30 minutes.

To prepare the barbecue sauce, combine the allspice, cloves, coriander, and vinegar in a saucepan and bring to a boil. Reduce the liquid by half, strain, and set aside. In a separate saucepan, heat the oil and sauté the garlic and onion over medium heat for 3 to 4 minutes. Add the brown sugar and cook the mixture for about 1 minute, or until the sugar melts. Add the molasses and Worcestershire sauce, and deglaze the pan with the beer. Stir in the chipotle chile puree and the reserved vinegar mixture, and simmer over low heat for 45 minutes. Stir in the ketchup and cook 15 minutes longer. Strain the mixture into a clean saucepan and keep warm over low heat, stirring occasionally.

Prepare the grill (or, alternatively, the steaks can be broiled or sautéed in a heavy pan or skillet using 1 tablespoon of hot olive oil or safflower oil; they will take approximately the same time to cook as they will on the grill).

While the sauce is cooking, prepare the potatoes. Place the potatoes in a saucepan with salted water and bring to a boil. Cook at a low boil for about 15 minutes, or until tender. Meanwhile, heat the milk, butter, red chile powder, and garlic in a saucepan. Drain the potatoes, place in a mixing bowl, and add the warm milk mixture. Mash together with an electric mixer, a potato masher, or a fork, leaving the potatoes smooth or lumpy, as you prefer. Season with salt and keep warm. Stir in the cilantro just before serving.

To cook the filets, rub the steaks lightly with the olive oil to prevent them from sticking to the grill. Grill the filets over medium-high heat for 5 to 6 minutes for medium-rare, or about 7 minutes per side for medium. Be careful not to have a high flame or the spice rub will easily burn.

To serve, spoon the barbecue sauce onto each warm serving plate. Place a filet in the center of the plate, spoon the mashed potatoes next to the steak, and serve immediately.

For the Potatoes:
1½ pounds new potatoes, diced
½ cup milk
2 tablespoons butter
2 teaspoons pure red chile
*   powder, or to taste*
2 cloves garlic, roasted and
*   mashed to a paste (page 189)*
Salt
1 teaspoon minced fresh cilantro

1 tablespoon olive oil

Bacon-Wrapped Beef Filets with Yucatan Oysters and Leeks

By Chef Mark Miller, Coyote Cafe, Santa Fe, New Mexico

For the Yucatan Oyster Sauce:

12 large fresh oysters, shucked
    and liquor reserved
1½ tablespoons black
    peppercorns
8 cloves garlic, roasted
    (page 189)
¼ teaspoon salt
1½ tablespoons olive oil
1 tablespoon freshly squeezed
    lime juice
4 cups beef stock (page 186)
1 tablespoon cumin, toasted and
    ground (page 189)
1 tablespoon toasted dried
    thyme (page 189)
2 tablespoons butter

For the Steaks:

4 aged center-cut beef filets,
    about 6 ounces each, at room
    temperature
4 slices pancetta or smoked
    bacon
Salt
Freshly ground black pepper
3 tablespoons olive oil

For the Leeks:

4 leeks, cut into thin julienne
    slices
2 tablespoons butter
Salt
Freshly ground black pepper

12 smoked oysters (optional)
1 cup Pico de Gallo Salsa
    (page 78; optional)

The starting point for the steaks in this recipe is a USDA prime or choice beef tenderloin with the tapered ends (head and tail) removed to assure a reasonably uniform steak shape and thickness. Aging beef naturally affects tenderness and flavor—enzymes produced by anaerobic bacteria break down muscle fibers while imparting an "aged" flavor to the meat—one that I far prefer to that of "fresh" meat. The sauce can be prepared ahead of time, and it's another fine example of the compatibility of steak and oysters (see also page 26). If you want to smoke your own oysters, use small Pacific types such as Hog Island or Kumamoto oysters. Cold-smoke them in the shell for 20 to 30 minutes or barbecue them over a very low covered fire with plenty of soaked wood chips for 10 to 15 minutes until the shells open slightly. In either case, make sure the oysters do not dry out or "boil" in their shells, and simply shuck them when they cool.

•••

To prepare the sauce, pour the oyster liquor from the shells into a sauté pan and bring to a boil. Add the oysters and poach gently over medium-low heat for about 2 minutes, until the edges begin to curl. Remove the oysters with a slotted spoon and set aside; reserve the cooking liquid in the pan.

Place the peppercorns, 2 garlic cloves, salt, and ½ cup of the hot oyster liquid in a blender and puree. Add the puree and oil to the liquid in the pan and bring to a boil. Remove from the heat and let cool.

Add the lime juice and reserved oysters to the mixture; puree again. Transfer the oyster puree to a saucepan and add the stock, cumin, thyme, and remaining garlic. Simmer for 20 minutes over low heat, then strain into a clean saucepan. Whisk in the butter until completely incorporated and set aside.

To prepare the steaks, wrap a bacon slice around each filet, securing with kitchen twine, and season with salt and pepper. Heat the oil in a heavy sauté pan or skillet to almost smoking. Lower the heat to medium and sear the steaks for 4 to 5 minutes per side; the filets should be crusty and browned on the outside and rare to medium-rare on the inside. If you prefer, cook about 1 minute longer on each side for medium-rare or about 2 minutes more per side for medium.

While the steaks are cooking, warm the oyster sauce.

To prepare the leeks, bring a saucepan of lightly salted water to a boil. Add the leeks and cook for 2 minutes. Drain carefully, toss in a bowl with the butter, and season with salt and pepper.

To serve, ladle the sauce on warm serving plates and place the steaks on top. Carefully cut the twine around the steaks and discard it. For each serving, divide the leeks into 3 portions around the beef and place a smoked oyster on top of each portion of leeks (3 per plate). Garnish the steaks with the salsa if desired.

Mark Miller was raised in New England and studied anthropology at the University of California, Berkeley, before starting his culinary career in 1976 with Alice Waters at Chez Panisse. He then opened two restaurants of his own in Berkeley, Fourth Street Grill and Santa Fe Bar and Grill, where he started cooking with southwestern ingredients and pioneering modern southwestern cuisine. Mark decided that the logical next step to develop his cooking style was to move to the Southwest; he opened Coyote Cafe in Santa Fe in 1987. Since then, Mark has opened two more Coyote Cafes—in Las Vegas, Nevada, and Austin, Texas. In 1992 Mark opened the western-themed Red Sage restaurant in Washington, D.C., where he also launched Raku, an Asian noodle restaurant, in 1996. Mark was named Best Chef in the Southwest region by the James Beard Foundation in 1996 and is a prolific author. He has written six cookbooks, including *Coyote Cafe, Coyote's Pantry, The Great Salsa Book*, and *Flavored Breads* (all published by Ten Speed Press), and has written and designed several food posters, including *The Great Chile Poster*.

Mesquite-Grilled Rib-eye Cowboy Steaks with Black Bean Rellenos and Pico de Gallo Salsa

SERVES 4

For the Pico de Gallo Salsa:
8 Roma tomatoes (about
   1 pound), diced
2 serrano chiles, minced (with
   seeds)
2 tablespoons finely diced red
   onion
2 tablespoons minced fresh
   cilantro
¼ cup Mexican beer, such as Dos
   Equis or Negra Modelo
Juice of 1 lime (about
   1 tablespoon)
1 teaspoon salt

For the Rellenos:
2 cups cooked black beans
1½ tablespoons canned chipotle
   chiles in adobo sauce
½ teaspoon cumin, toasted and
   ground (page 189)
Pinch of salt
4 green New Mexico or Anaheim
   chiles, roasted and peeled,
   stems left intact
4 eggs, beaten
1 tablespoon milk
1 cup all-purpose flour, for
   dusting
2 cups cornmeal
Pinch of salt
Pinch of cayenne
Peanut oil

This is hearty, stick-to-the-ribs cowboy fare and a must for meat lovers. A version of this recipe has been on the menu at Coyote Cafe in Santa Fe since the restaurant opened in 1987. In some markets you'll find this cut of meat sold as a bone-in Delmonico steak, and for a more elegant look you can trim off all the fat from the "eye."

Rellenos are stuffed green chiles that are deep-fried, and in the Southwest you'll usually find them filled with cheese. In some parts of Mexico, dry as well as fresh chiles are sometimes stuffed to make rellenos using picadillo, a savory meat filling. But here we use another southwestern classic: black beans accented with the smoky flavor of chipotle chiles. Chipotles are smoked, dried jalapeño chiles that are available either dehydrated or canned in adobo sauce, a vinegar and tomato-based stew. For sources of chipotle chiles in adobo sauce, see the Resource Guide (page 190).

••

Thoroughly combine all the ingredients for the salsa in a mixing bowl. Let sit at room temperature for up to 2 hours until ready to serve. (Keep refrigerated if making further ahead of time and bring to room temperature before serving.)

Prepare the grill (or, alternatively, the steaks can be broiled).

To prepare the rellenos, place the beans, chipotle chiles, cumin, and salt in a food processor and puree until smooth. Set aside. Leaving the stems intact, carefully make a lengthwise slit in the roasted chiles and remove the seeds and ribs. Spoon the pureed filling into the chiles, being careful not to overstuff or rip the chiles.

Mix the eggs and milk together in a shallow bowl or soup plate to form an egg wash. Place the flour and the cornmeal mixed with the salt and cayenne on separate plates. Dredge the stuffed chiles in the flour, shaking off any excess, then dip them

into the egg wash, letting the excess drip off. Finally, dredge the chiles in the cornmeal and coat well.

Heat the oil in a deep fryer or heavy-bottomed deep skillet to 350 degrees. Carefully place the chiles in the hot oil and fry for about 45 seconds to 1 minute, until golden brown. Remove from the oil and place on a platter lined with paper towels to drain. Keep warm in a low oven.

To prepare the steaks, season with salt and pepper. Grill the steaks for 6 to 7 minutes per side for medium-rare or 8 to 9 minutes per side for medium, depending on the heat of the grill and the thickness of the steaks.

Place the steaks on warm serving plates and top with the Pico de Gallo salsa. Place a black bean relleno next to each steak, garnish the plate with a cilantro sprig, and serve immediately.

For the Cowboy Steaks:
4 bone-in rib-eye steaks, 16 to 18 ounces each, about 1 to 1½ inches thick, left at room temperature for 1 hour before cooking
Salt
Freshly cracked black pepper

4 sprigs fresh cilantro, for garnish

Coriander-Cured Filets with Sweet Onion Confit and Green Chile Spoon Bread

By Chef Stephan Pyles, Star Canyon, Dallas, Texas

SERVES 4

For the Coriander Cure:

¼ cup coriander seeds

¼ cup black peppercorns

4 shallots, minced

4 garlic cloves, minced

¾ cup kosher salt or ½ cup table salt

6 tablespoons dark brown sugar

¼ cup olive oil

For the Steaks:

4 filet mignon steaks, about 7 or 8 ounces each

For the Green Chile Spoon Bread:

¾ cup corn kernels (cut from 1 large ear)

¾ cup milk

¾ cup chicken stock

½ cup cornmeal

1½ teaspoons salt, or more to taste

¼ teaspoon freshly ground white pepper

2 tablespoons butter

2 teaspoons pureed roasted garlic (page 189)

1 large poblano chile, 2 green New Mexico chiles, or 3 to 4 jalapeño chiles, roasted, peeled, seeded, and diced (page 189)

1 serrano chile, seeded and minced

3 tablespoons diced green bell pepper

3 tablespoons diced red bell pepper

½ cup heavy cream

3 eggs, separated

Marinating meat with this coriander-based cure gives it a wonderful southwestern-range flavor, and I like to prepare whole beef tenderloins or venison loins the same way. The thick, sweet onion confit complements the texture and flavor of the cured meat perfectly. The elegant southern tradition of spoon bread is given a southwestern twist here with the addition of the chiles. Texas cuisine is influenced by the cooking of many other regions and countries, especially the American South and Mexico. Spoon bread is believed to have been derived originally from the Native American suppone, a porridgelike dish. My version has a rich texture, rather like a soufflé, and it can be used to accompany other dark meats or game with great results.

—*Stephan*

• •

To prepare the cure, place the coriander seeds and peppercorns in a food processor and pulse for about 1 minute, until coarsely ground. Add the shallots, garlic, salt, and sugar, and pulse together. With the machine running, add the oil in a slow, steady stream until the mixture forms a thick paste. Transfer this coriander cure to a shallow dish, add the steaks, and coat completely. Cover with plastic wrap and refrigerate for at least 30 minutes, turning the meat occasionally.

Preheat the oven to 325 degrees. Lightly oil a 1- to 1½-quart baking dish or soufflé dish or individual 6-ounce ramekins.

To prepare the spoon bread, place the corn in a single layer in a hot, dry, heavy cast-iron skillet. Dry-roast for 4 to 5 minutes, tossing continuously, until scorched and dark. Set aside. Combine the milk and stock in a large saucepan and bring to a boil over high heat. Boil the mixture for 30 seconds, then lower the heat to medium. Whisk in the cornmeal until smooth. Remove the pan from the heat and stir in the salt, pepper, and butter until thoroughly combined. Transfer to a large mixing bowl and stir in the roasted corn, garlic, chiles, bell peppers, and cream until thoroughly mixed together. Set aside to cool slightly.

Whisk the egg yolks into the mixture. Beat the egg whites to soft peaks and gently fold in. Pour the mixture into the prepared dish or ramekins, three-quarters full, and place inside a water bath or larger pan. Add enough very hot water to the water bath to come about 1 inch up the side of the spoon bread dish. Transfer to the oven and bake for 35 to 45 minutes (depending on whether you are using a dish or ramekins), or until a knife inserted in the center comes out clean. Check the spoon bread after the first 25 to 30 minutes; if it is browning too quickly, cover with aluminum foil. Serve hot from the oven.

Meanwhile, prepare the onion confit. Melt the butter in a heavy sauté pan or skillet, add the onions to the hot pan, and sauté over medium-high heat for 1 minute. Add the sugar and sauté just until dissolved. Deglaze the pan with the vinegars and cook the mixture for 3 to 5 minutes, until the liquid has evaporated. Season with salt and keep warm.

Heat the vegetable oil in a heavy sauté pan or skillet until lightly smoking. Remove the steaks from the cure and scrape off any excess. Season with salt and pepper and sear in the pan over

For the Sweet Onion Confit:
1 tablespoon butter
1 cup sliced sweet onions, such as Texas Spring Sweet, Noonday, or Vidalia
2 tablespoons sugar
2 tablespoons white wine vinegar
2 tablespoons red wine vinegar
Salt

3 tablespoons vegetable oil
Salt
Freshly ground black pepper
4 sprigs fresh sage, for garnish

Coriander-Cured Filet with
Sweet Onion Confit and
Green Chile Spoon Bread

medium-high heat for 5 to 6 minutes on each side for medium-rare or 7 to 8 minutes per side for medium.

To serve, place each filet in the center of a warm serving plate and top with the onion confit. Serve the hot spoon bread next to the steak, garnish with the sage, and serve immediately.

Spice-Rubbed Sirloin Steaks with Chorizo Potato Hash and Golden Tomato Sauce

SERVES 4

For the Steaks:
3 tablespoons cumin seeds
2 tablespoons dried oregano
½ tablespoon black peppercorns
¼ teaspoon salt
4 top sirloin steaks, about
    10 ounces each
1 tablespoon olive oil

For the Golden Tomato Sauce:
1 pound yellow tomatoes,
    chopped
3 cloves garlic, roasted (page 189)
2 teaspoons chopped ginger
½ teaspoon sugar
¼ teaspoon salt
2 teaspoons store-bought
    habanero chile sauce
2 teaspoons pureed canned
    chipotle chile
1½ tablespoons fresh lime juice

For the Hash:
1 pound new potatoes, quartered
8 ounces hard Spanish-style
    chorizo or andouille sausage
1 tablespoon olive oil
2 shallots, minced
1 garlic clove, minced
½ cup sun-dried tomatoes
    packed in oil, drained
1 teaspoon chopped fresh
    marjoram
1 teaspoon sherry vinegar
    (optional)
Salt

4 sprigs fresh cilantro, for garnish

Here is another example of the technique of rubbing steak with a dry marinade to enhance its natural flavor. In this case, the mixture of toasted cumin, oregano, and black pepper lends the sirloin a hint of the outdoors and open range, giving a sense of the essence that lies behind the tradition and origin of many southwestern dishes.

The chorizo used in the rustic potato hash in this recipe refers to the hard Spanish-style sausage rather than the crumbly, piquant Mexican-style chorizo sausage. The Cajun-style andouille sausage is a good substitute.

The visually striking sauce catches the eye, while the unexpected combination of chiles and ginger that it contains intrigues the palate.

• •

Combine the cumin, oregano, peppercorns, and salt in a dry skillet and toast over medium heat for about 2 minutes, until fragrant. Transfer the mixture to a spice grinder and pulse until finely ground. Massage the spice mixture into the steaks, transfer to a platter, cover with plastic wrap, and let sit at room temperature for 30 minutes.

To prepare the sauce, place all the ingredients in a food processor or blender and puree until smooth. Transfer to a saucepan, heat through, and keep warm.

Prepare the grill (or, alternatively, the steaks can be broiled).

Bring a saucepan of salted water to a boil. Add the potatoes and blanch for 5 minutes. Drain and set aside.

Quarter the chorizo by cutting in half lengthwise and then in half crosswise. Heat the oil in a large, heavy skillet. Add the sausage and sauté over medium heat for 2 to 3 minutes, until it begins to render a little fat. Add the shallots, garlic, and sun-dried tomatoes, and sauté for 1 minute. Add the potatoes and combine the mixture thoroughly. Sauté about 3 minutes longer, or until the

potatoes are tender. Stir in the marjoram, vinegar, and salt, and cover to keep warm.

Rub the steaks lightly with the oil to prevent them from sticking to the grill, and lightly oil the rack of the grill. Place the steaks over a medium-high fire and grill for about 5 minutes per side for medium-rare or about 6 to 7 minutes per side for medium. Be careful not to have a high flame or the rub will easily burn.

To serve, place the hash at the top of warm serving plates. Lean the steaks against the hash and spoon the sauce around the steaks. Garnish with a cilantro sprig and serve immediately.

Spice-Rubbed Sirloin Steak with
Chorizo Potato Hash and
Golden Tomato Sauce

Pan-Seared Strip Steaks with Chipotle Butter and Twice-Baked Potatoes

By Chef Bobby Flay, Mesa Grill, New York, New York

For the Twice-Baked Potatoes:

6 russet potatoes
8 ounces soft goat cheese
½ cup thinly sliced scallions
2 tablespoons pureed canned
    chipotle chiles
2 tablespoons butter
½ cup milk or low-fat milk
Salt
Freshly ground white pepper

For the Chipotle Butter:

8 tablespoons (1 stick) butter
1 canned chipotle chile in adobo
    sauce
1 garlic clove
2 tablespoons chopped red
    onion
Salt
Freshly ground black pepper

For the Steaks:

6 boneless strip steaks, about
    10 ounces each
2 tablespoons ground cumin
Salt
Freshly ground black pepper
½ cup olive oil

You may want to use two skillets to sear the steaks to speed the cooking process; and you can cook two steaks in each skillet. You can also grill the steaks, but pan-searing in a little olive oil gives the steaks a crisp crust that seals in all their juices. For best results let the steaks rest briefly before serving. The savory stuffed potatoes are perfect with steak, and the chiles add a surprising dimension of flavor. Serve with a mixed green salad of your choice.

—*Bobby*

• •

Preheat the oven to 350 degrees.

Wrap the potatoes in foil and bake in the oven for 1 hour, or until tender. Remove the foil and let cool to room temperature. When cool enough to handle, cut off ¼ inch from each end of the potatoes and carefully hollow them out, leaving the skin intact.

Place the potato flesh in a mixing bowl and mash with the goat cheese, scallions, and chipotle puree.

Heat the butter and milk in a small saucepan until hot and the butter has melted. Beat into the potato-cheese mixture and season with salt and pepper. Stuff the potato skins with the potato mixture. (You can prepare the potatoes up to this point ahead of time and keep them in the refrigerator. Bring to room temperature before reheating.) When ready to serve, heat the oven to 400 degrees, place the stuffed potatoes on a baking sheet, and bake for 5 minutes, until hot.

While the potatoes are baking, place all the ingredients for the chipotle butter in a food processor. Process the mixture until completely incorporated. Transfer the mixture to a long sheet of parchment or wax paper and shape the mixture into a cylinder about 1 inch in diameter, following the long side of the paper. Leave about a 1-inch border between the butter and the edge of the paper. Roll the butter up in the paper to form a log and refrigerate for at least 30 minutes. (You may refrigerate the butter up to 3 days or freeze it.)

Season the steaks with the ground cumin, salt, and pepper. Heat the oil in a heavy cast-iron skillet over high heat until the oil begins to smoke. Add the steaks to the hot pan and sear on the first side for about 4 minutes. Turn over and sear on the other side for about 4 minutes for medium-rare. Cook 1 or 2 minutes longer on each side for medium.

To serve, remove the steaks from the pan and place in the center of warm serving plates. Cut 6 slices from the log of butter, each about ½ inch thick, and place 1 slice of the butter on each of the steaks. Serve immediately with a baked stuffed potato.

Flame-haired **Bobby Flay** fell into cooking at the age of seventeen when he took a job at Joe Allen's restaurant in Manhattan. He impressed the restaurant's management sufficiently that they paid his tuition at the prestigious French Culinary Institute. Renowned chef Jonathan Waxman first introduced Bobby to the southwestern ingredients that were to change his cooking forever, and Bobby was instantly drawn to indigenous American foods. From 1988 to 1990 Bobby developed his southwestern cooking at the Miracle Grill in Manhattan, and in 1991 he opened Mesa Grill to rave reviews. He was voted Rising Star Chef of the Year by the James Beard Foundation in 1993, and the following year his first book, *Bold American Food,* was published by Warner Books; the book won the Institute of American Culinary Professionals' Award for design. In 1993 Bobby opened his second (Spanish-themed) restaurant, Bolo, with partner Laurence Kretchmer, and in 1996 his latest venture, Mesa City, opened on Manhattan's Upper East Side.

Steak Fajitas with Black Beans and Spicy Red Rice

SERVES 4

For the Marinade:
1 bottle dark beer, such as Negra
    Modelo or Dos Equis
1 jalapeño chile, minced
6 scallions, sliced
2 garlic cloves, minced
2 tablespoons soy sauce
¼ cup chopped fresh cilantro
Pinch of ground cumin
Pinch of ground dried oregano

For the Steaks:
4 top sirloin steaks, about
    8 ounces each, sliced into
    thin strips about 2 to 3 inches
    long and ½ inch wide

3 cups cooked black beans
    (page 188)

For the Spicy Red Rice:
½ teaspoon dried ground
    oregano
½ teaspoon ground cumin
3 tablespoons butter
2 garlic cloves, minced
½ onion, minced
1½ cups white rice, rinsed in
    cold water and drained
1½ tablespoons pure red chile
    powder
¾ teaspoon salt

Fajitas means "belts" in Spanish, referring to the strips of meat that are usually marinated and grilled. Although the popular fajitas are often thought of as Mexican, they originated in the San Antonio region of Texas during the 1800s. The flavor of fajitas will be enhanced if you plan ahead and marinate them overnight. Here we use sirloin rather than the traditional skirt steak, which is a tougher cut; leaner cuts are typically used for especially tender, tasty fajitas. If you cannot find a smoky barbecue sauce, use a regular sauce and add a tablespoon of puréed chipotle chiles in adobo sauce (see page 78). To simplify this recipe, serve this dish with just flour tortillas rather than rice; you can also substitute guacamole, diced tomatoes, or Pico de Gallo salsa (page 78) for the beans. Serve with grated cheese and chopped onion on the side if you wish.

∙∙∙

Thoroughly mix together all the marinade ingredients in a glass dish. Add the sliced sirloin and toss together to coat thoroughly. Cover and marinate for at least 4 hours and preferably overnight in the refrigerator. Remove the dish from the refrigerator and let sit at room temperature for at least 1 hour before cooking.

Prepare the beans and keep warm.

To prepare the rice, place the oregano and cumin in a dry, heavy skillet and toast over low heat, stirring frequently, for about 1 minute, until fragrant. Set aside.

Melt the butter in a sauté pan or skillet. Add the garlic and onion, and sauté over medium-low heat for 7 or 8 minutes, until soft. Stir in the rice, 3½ cups of water, chile powder, and salt, and bring to a boil. Cook for 2 minutes, lower the heat to a simmer, and cover the pan. Simmer the rice for 20 to 25 minutes, until the liquid is absorbed. Remove the pan from the heat and let stand for 5 minutes. Keep warm. Fluff with a fork before serving.

To prepare the fajitas, heat the oil in a heavy-bottomed skillet. Remove the meat from the marinade, drain, and pat dry. Place the marinated steak in the hot pan and sauté for 2 to 3 minutes, stirring frequently, until browned. Remove the meat from the pan and keep warm. Add the onion, poblano chile, and red bell pepper to the same pan, season with salt and pepper, and sauté over medium-high heat for 3 to 4 minutes, until soft. Add the sautéed steak, orange juice, and lime juice, and toss together.

Warm the tortillas on a griddle or in a dry skillet. Place in a basket and cover with a towel to keep warm. Place the fajita mixture in the center of a large serving platter. Place the beans and rice in separate serving dishes and garnish with cilantro.

To serve, the guests should transfer some of the rice and beans to their plates. Then they should take a warm tortilla, place some of the fajita mixture in the center, and garnish with the sour cream and cilantro. A little of the avocado and a sprinkling with a lime wedge should be added. After the tortilla has been rolled up, it can be eaten by hand. (Serve 2 tortillas per person.)

For the Fajitas:
2 tablespoons peanut oil
1 red onion, sliced
1 poblano chile or green bell pepper, seeded and julienned
1 red bell pepper, seeded and julienned
Salt
Freshly ground black pepper
Juice of 1 orange
Juice of 1 lime
8 flour tortillas

For the Garnish:
Chopped fresh cilantro leaves
¼ cup (4 tablespoons) sour cream
1 avocado, pitted, quartered, and sliced
1 lime, cut into wedges

Beef Tenderloin Marinated in Molasses and Black Pepper with a Wild Mushroom, Bacon, and Sweet Potato Compote

By Chef Dean Fearing, The Mansion on Turtle Creek, Dallas, Texas

SERVES 4

For the Marinade:

1 cup dark molasses
2 tablespoons balsamic vinegar
2 tablespoons freshly cracked black pepper
2 garlic cloves, minced
1 large shallot, minced
2 teaspoons finely grated ginger
1 teaspoon minced fresh thyme
2 teaspoons crushed red pepper flakes, or to taste

For the Beef:

2 pounds center-cut beef tenderloin, trimmed of all fat and silver skin

For the Glazed Pecans:

½ cup water
½ cup sugar
2 dried red chiles, such as cayenne, de arbol, or chiltepin
1 cup whole shelled pecans
¼ cup dark molasses

Salt

This is an elegant way to serve beef that befits the award-winning Mansion on Turtle Creek. The rich and hearty flavors of the molasses and balsamic vinegar–marinated beef are unusual. Pecans are a southern crop and popular in Texas, and the glazed pecans can be made independently of this recipe and served as a tasty snack.

• •

Thoroughly combine the marinade ingredients in a large glass dish. Add the tenderloin, cover the dish, and refrigerate for 24 hours, turning the meat occasionally.

Preheat the oven to 250 degrees.

To prepare the pecans, combine the water, sugar, and chiles in a small saucepan and bring to a boil over high heat. Add the pecans and return to a boil. Turn the heat to low and simmer the pecans for 10 minutes. Drain the pecans and spread them out on a baking sheet. Bake in the oven for 45 minutes, stirring occasionally. Remove the pecans from the oven and transfer to a small bowl. Add the molasses and toss to coat. Return the pecans to the baking sheet and bake in the oven 45 minutes longer, until very crispy but not burned. Remove from the oven and let cool.

Meanwhile, remove the tenderloin from the marinade and reserve ½ cup of the marinade for the compote and another ¼ cup to deglaze the pan. Place the tenderloin on a cutting board and, using a sharp knife, slice the meat into 8 medallions. Season each medallion with salt and set aside.

To prepare the compote, heat the stock in a saucepan and bring to a boil. Mix the cornstarch and water in a cup and add to the stock, whisking constantly. Lower the heat and simmer the stock until 1 cup remains; it should be thick enough to coat the back of a spoon. Meanwhile, place the reserved ½ cup of marinade in a separate saucepan and reduce over medium-high heat for 5 minutes, or until reduced by half. Add the reduced stock to the reduced marinade and bring the mixture to a boil. Lower the heat and simmer for 5 minutes, or until it again coats the back of a spoon. Turn off the heat and cover to keep warm.

Place the bacon in a sauté pan and sauté over medium-high heat for 5 to 7 minutes, or until golden brown. Drain on paper towels and reserve. Clean the pan with a paper towel and heat the oil. Add the mushrooms to the hot pan and sauté over medium-high heat for 3 minutes, or until tender. Remove the mushrooms from the pan and reserve.

Preheat the oven to 350 degrees.

Cut the sweet potato in half and, using a Parisian scoop or melon baller, scoop out 1 cup of sweet potato balls. Melt the butter in a heavy ovenproof skillet or sauté pan over medium heat. Add the potato balls and pearl onions to the hot butter and sauté for 3 minutes. Stir in the brown sugar and vinegar, and sauté 2 minutes longer. Transfer the pan to the oven and bake for about 7 minutes, stirring occasionally to glaze evenly. Remove the pan from the oven, stir in the rendered bacon, sautéed mushrooms, the reduced stock mixture, and the glazed pecans. Season with salt and lemon juice, and keep warm over very low heat.

(continued)

For the Compote:
3 cups beef stock (page 186)
1 tablespoon cornstarch
1 tablespoon cold water
1 cup diced smoked bacon
1 tablespoon vegetable oil
2 cups sliced wild mushrooms, such as morels, chanterelles, or shiitakes
1 large sweet potato
2 tablespoons butter
½ cup peeled pearl onions
1 tablespoon brown sugar
2 teaspoons cider vinegar
Salt
Freshly squeezed lemon juice

2 tablespoons vegetable oil
4 sprigs fresh watercress, for garnish

Heat the oil in a large cast-iron skillet or sauté pan. Add the beef medallions to the hot pan and brown for 3 minutes. Turn the meat over and brown on the other side for 2 minutes, or to the desired doneness. Just before removing the meat, add the reserved ¼ cup of the marinade to deglaze the pan and to glaze the medallions. Quickly turn the meat over to glaze the other side and immediately remove from the pan.

To serve, place 2 beef medallions in the center of each warm serving plate. Spoon the compote next to the medallions, letting it flow out onto the plate. Place a sprig of watercress in between the meat and the compote, and serve immediately.

Dean Fearing was born in Louisville, Kentucky, and trained at the Culinary Institute of America in New York. He began his professional career at Maisonette in Cincinnati before moving on to The Pyramid Room at the Fairmont Hotel in Dallas. Dean went to The Mansion on Turtle Creek as executive sous chef when it opened in 1980. He left to become chef and part-owner of Agnew's restaurant but returned to The Mansion in 1985 as executive chef. Dean enjoys cooking southwestern foods with seasonal local and native ingredients complemented by an array of flavors from around the world, notably Italy, Thailand, Mexico, and the American South. Dean was named the Best Chef in the Southwest for 1994 by the James Beard Foundation, and he has written two cookbooks, *The Mansion on Turtle Creek Cookbook* and *Dean Fearing's Southwest Cuisine: Blending Asia and the Americas*.

Seared Beef Filets with Drunken Beans and Smoky Tomatillo Sauce

SERVES 4

For the Borracho Beans:
1 cup dried pinto beans, picked through, rinsed, and soaked overnight
1 tablespoon olive oil
3 tablespoons finely diced onion
5 serrano chiles, seeded and minced
1 pound Roma tomatoes, diced
⅔ cup (½ bottle) dark beer, such as Negra Modelo
Salt
2 tablespoons chopped fresh cilantro

For the Smoky Tomatillo Sauce:
1 pound tomatillos, husked and rinsed
1 large clove garlic, roasted (page 189)
Pinch of sugar
Pinch of salt
2 tablespoons canned chipotle chiles in adobo sauce
¼ cup coarsely chopped fresh cilantro leaves

For the Steaks:
4 filet mignon steaks, about 6 ounces each
Salt
Freshly ground black pepper
2 tablespoons olive oil

8 corn tortillas
4 ounces queso fresco or other dry cheese such as Monterey Jack, grated
4 sprigs fresh cilantro, for garnish

The poetically named "drunken" beans are so called because they are cooked in beer, a recipe derived from "norteño," or northern Mexican cooking, where they are called "borracho" beans. It's the chipotle chiles that give the sauce its deliciously smoky quality (for notes on chipotles in adobo sauce, see page 78). Tomatillos are common ingredients in southwestern cuisine, and they are widely available in cities around the country that have Hispanic or Caribbean populations. Tomatillos look like green tomatoes and belong to the same family, but they are more closely related to the Cape gooseberry, which also has a thin, papery, parchmentlike covering. The citrusy green apple flavor of tomatillos is transformed by blackening them, giving them robust, complex tones. If you use less water in the sauce to leave it thicker, you can make a great dipping salsa for chips.

· ·

To prepare the beans, drain and rinse the pintos and transfer to a saucepan. Add enough water to the saucepan to cover the beans by 1 or 2 inches. Bring the beans to a boil, then turn the heat to low. Cook at a low simmer for about 1½ to 2 hours, until the beans are just tender. Add more water as the beans cook to keep them covered. Drain the beans and set aside.

Heat the oil in a large sauté pan. Add the onion and serrano chiles, and sauté over medium heat for about 5 minutes, or until soft. Stir in the tomatoes, cooked beans, and beer. Season with salt and bring the mixture to a boil. Lower the heat to a simmer and cook the mixture for 10 to 15 minutes, until the liquid thickens. Keep warm and stir in the cilantro just before serving.

(continued)

To prepare the tomatillo sauce, blacken the tomatillos under a broiler or over a gas flame, turning frequently; do not overblacken or they will become bitter. Coarsely chop the tomatillos, and place in a food processor or blender. Add the garlic, sugar, salt, and ¼ cup of water, and puree until smooth. Add the chipotle chiles and cilantro, and pulse until smooth. Add a little more water to thin if necessary. Just before serving, transfer the mixture to a saucepan and heat through.

Season the filets with salt and pepper. Heat the oil in a large, heavy sauté pan or skillet. Add the filets to the hot pan and sear over high heat for 3 to 4 minutes per side for medium-rare or 4 to 5 minutes per side for medium. Remove the filets from the pan and keep warm.

Soften the tortillas by placing them in a shallow bowl of warm water for a few seconds. Place the tortillas, one by one, in the same pan used for cooking the filets and warm them over medium heat, turning once. Place 2 tortillas on each warm serving plate. Spoon the beans in the center of each tortilla and place the seared filets next to the beans. Spoon the sauce generously over the filets and sprinkle with the cheese. Garnish with the cilantro and serve immediately.

Seared Beef Filet with
Drunken Beans and
Smoky Tomatillo Sauce

5

California,
the West Coast,
and
Hawaii

Gilroy Garlic Confit Steaks with Artichoke-Orzo Ragout

SERVES 4

For the Garlic Confit:
3 heads garlic, cloves peeled
1 sprig fresh rosemary
1 small dried red chile (such as
    chile de arbol or cayenne) or
    8 black peppercorns
1½ cups olive oil

For the Artichoke-Orzo Ragout:
12 baby artichokes, outer leaves
    trimmed off
1 lemon, cut in half
2 tablespoons olive oil
1 small white onion, sliced
¼ cup sun-dried tomatoes
    packed in oil, drained and
    sliced
1 tablespoon red wine vinegar
¼ cup vegetable or chicken stock
1 cup cooked orzo pasta
Salt
Freshly ground black pepper
1 tablespoon sliced fresh basil

For the Steaks:
4 filet mignon steaks,
    7 or 8 ounces each
Salt
Freshly ground black pepper

2 tablespoons grated Parmesan
    cheese (optional)
4 lemon wedges, for garnish
4 thick slices French bread, cut
    on a diagonal (optional)

Gilroy is to garlic as Yankee Stadium is to baseball or Terlingua, Texas, is to chili: It is the self-proclaimed garlic capital of the world. Every summer the community of Gilroy, which lies some eighty miles south of San Francisco and forty miles east of Santa Cruz in northern California, holds a huge garlic festival. If you happen to be a garlic lover and relish such delicacies as garlic soup and garlic ice cream, this is one event you won't want to miss! Here we offer a confit of garlic. This classic French technique was originally a means of preserving meats, especially goose or duck, by rendering them slowly and storing them in their own fat. Since garlic has no fat, we help it along with olive oil. The resulting smooth and deliciously flavored puree can also be used to spread on bread for crostini, for making flavored croutons, or as a sandwich spread. Orzo is small, grain-sized pasta (the word means "barley" in Italian).

• •

Place all the garlic confit ingredients in a small saucepan. Bring to a simmer over low heat and cook gently for 1 hour. Let cool. When cool, remove the rosemary and chile, and discard. Transfer the garlic and oil to a food processor or blender and puree until smooth. Set aside.

Prepare the grill. (Or, alternatively, the steaks can be broiled or sautéed in a heavy pan or skillet using 1 tablespoon of hot olive oil or safflower oil. They will take approximately the same time to cook as they will on the grill.)

To prepare the ragout, rub the trimmed artichokes with the lemon halves to prevent discoloration. Place in a steamer or steamer basket set over a saucepan of boiling water and steam for 8 to 10 minutes, or until tender. Let cool slightly and cut into quarters. Heat the oil in a sauté pan. Add the onion and sauté over high heat for 2 to 3 minutes, or until the onion has turned translucent and is just beginning to brown at the edges. Lower

the heat to medium-high, add the artichokes and sun-dried tomatoes, and sauté 1 minute longer. Stir in the vinegar and stock, and bring the mixture to a simmer. Stir in the cooked orzo and heat through for about 1 minute. Season the ragout with salt and pepper, and cover to keep warm. Stir in the basil just before serving.

To prepare the steaks, season each filet with salt and pepper, and rub with the garlic confit. Place on the medium-hot grill and grill for 5 to 6 minutes per side for medium-rare or about 8 minutes per side for medium.

To serve, spoon a large mound of the ragout on each warm serving plate and sprinkle the grated cheese over the top, if desired. Place the steaks on top of the ragout. Garnish each serving with a lemon wedge and a slice of bread spread with some of the remaining garlic confit, if desired, and serve immediately.

Sliced Sirloin Steak with Sun-dried Tomatoes and California Goat Cheese, and a Napa Valley Mustard Sauce

SERVES 4

For the Mustard Sauce:
⅓ cup heavy cream
⅓ cup sour cream
3 tablespoons drained prepared
    horseradish
2 tablespoons Dijon or whole-
    grain mustard
Pinch of salt

For the Croutons:
8 slices French bread, about
    ½ inch thick
½ tablespoon olive oil

For the Steaks:
½ teaspoon salt
1 teaspoon freshly ground black
    pepper
¾ teaspoon fennel seeds
¾ teaspoon dried thyme
4 top sirloin steaks, about
    8 ounces each

For the Balsamic-Garlic Vinaigrette:
2 tablespoons olive oil
1 teaspoon minced garlic
3 tablespoons balsamic vinegar

Napa Valley in northern California is renowned for its fine vineyards but is less well known for its mustard crop. In the summer, fields are ablaze with bright yellow mustard flowers, and every year Napa holds a mustard festival. This recipe showcases mustard as well as the versatility of goat cheese; some of the first goat cheeses made commercially in the United States in the 1970s were produced in California.

The mixed baby lettuces featured in this salad are often marketed as a mesclun mix. This style of salad has become popular in the United States, but it is typical of southern France; the word "mesclun" means "mix" in the dialect of that region.

• •

Preheat the oven to 350 degrees and prepare the grill (or, alternatively, the steaks can be broiled).

To prepare the mustard sauce, whip the cream in a mixing bowl to soft peaks. Whisk in the sour cream, horseradish, mustard, and salt until thoroughly blended (overmixing will deflate the heavy cream). Refrigerate until ready to serve.

To prepare the croutons, lightly brush both sides of the bread with oil and cut neatly into cubes. Place on a baking sheet and toast in the oven for about 10 minutes, until crisp and golden brown. Remove from the oven and let cool.

Place the salt, pepper, fennel seeds, and thyme in a heavy-bottomed skillet and toast lightly over medium heat for about 1 minute, until just fragrant. Transfer to a spice grinder and grind to a powder. Rub the mixture onto the steaks. Grill the seasoned steaks for 4 to 5 minutes per side for medium-rare and about 6 minutes per side for medium. Remove the steaks from the grill and let rest for 5 minutes before slicing.

While the steaks are grilling, prepare the vinaigrette: Whisk together the oil, garlic, and vinegar until emulsified. Set aside.

To prepare the salad, place the slices of goat cheese on a plate and sprinkle with oil and pepper. Thoroughly mix together the bread crumbs and herbs in a mixing bowl. Dredge the cheese slices in the bread crumb mixture, coating thoroughly. Transfer the slices to a baking sheet and bake in the oven for 5 minutes. Meanwhile, toss the lettuces with the vinaigrette in a mixing bowl.

To serve, place a mound of lettuce on one side of each serving plate and top with the baked goat cheese slices, croutons, and tomatoes. Ladle the chilled mustard sauce on the other side of each plate and arrange the steak slices on top of the sauce. Serve immediately.

For the Salad:
8 ounces fresh goat cheese, cut into 8 slices
¼ cup olive oil
Freshly cracked black pepper
1 cup fine bread crumbs
1 teaspoon dried herbes de Provence, or mixed dried herbs
4 to 5 ounces mixed baby lettuces, such as red oak, arugula, frisée, and radicchio

8 sun-dried tomatoes packed in oil, drained

Oven-Roasted Strip Steak with Wild Onion and Chanterelle Compote

By Chef Bradley Ogden, One Market Restaurant, San Francisco, California

SERVES 8

For the Chanterelle Butter:
1½ cups thinly sliced chanterelle
   mushrooms, with stems on
¾ cup dry white wine
1 tablespoon tarragon vinegar
¼ cup minced shallots
1 teaspoon minced garlic
½ teaspoon kosher salt
1 teaspoon freshly cracked black
   pepper
4 tablespoons butter, softened

For the Beef:
1 boneless New York strip roast,
   about 2 ½ pounds
1 teaspoon kosher salt
½ teaspoon freshly cracked
   black pepper

For the Wild Onion Compote:
⅓ cup butter or olive oil
2 pounds chanterelles, oyster
   mushrooms, or shiitakes,
   cleaned and trimmed
24 wild onions or scallions,
   sliced into long strips
4 red bell peppers, seeded and
   julienned
1 tablespoon minced garlic
3 serrano chiles, seeded and
   julienned
Salt
Freshly ground black pepper

1 cup beef stock (page 186)

If you have a roasting spit, this recipe is the perfect opportunity to use it. If you'd like to serve a starch with this dish, Bradley suggests mashed red new potatoes with garlic: Boil small red potatoes and purée them with the cloves from a whole head of garlic that are simmered with 1 cup of milk, 1 cup of cream, and ¼ cup of butter until tender (add the simmered liquid to mash the potatoes).

The wild onions that he calls for, also known as ramps or wild leeks, have a strong flavor somewhere between onions and garlic, and are available at specialty produce markets in the spring. They make a wonderful addition to the chanterelle compote, but scallions make an acceptable substitute.

• •

Preheat the oven to 400 degrees.

To prepare the chanterelle butter, combine the mushrooms, wine, vinegar, shallots, garlic, salt, and pepper in a saucepan. Simmer the mixture over medium-low heat until the mushrooms are tender and the liquid is almost completely absorbed. Remove from the heat and let cool. Transfer to a food processor, add the butter, and blend until smooth. Set aside.

Rub the beef roast with the salt and pepper. Place in a roasting pan (or mount on a roasting spit) and roast in the oven for about 1 hour, or until an internal temperature of 120 degrees is reached, for medium-rare. Remove the meat from the oven (or spit) and let rest, loosely covered, for 20 minutes.

To prepare the compote, melt the butter or oil in a large skillet over high heat. Add the mushrooms to the hot pan and sauté for 1 minute. Add the onions, bell peppers, garlic, and serranos, and sauté for 1 or 2 minutes, or until the vegetables are tender. Season with salt and pepper, and transfer the mixture to a serving bowl. Cover to keep warm.

Return the same pan to high heat and deglaze with the stock. Quickly reduce by half over high heat. Remove the pan from the heat and whisk ½ cup of the chanterelle butter and any juices from the meat into the sauce.

To serve, cut the meat into thin slices and place on warm serving plates. Top with the compote, spoon the sauce all around, and serve immediately.

Bradley Ogden grew up in Michigan and trained professionally at the Culinary Institute of America where he received the school award for "most likely to succeed." In 1979 he was hired as sous chef at The American Restaurant in Kansas City and was promoted to executive chef within six months. Bradley moved to San Francisco as the executive chef of the newly opened Campton Place Hotel restaurant, and in 1989 he left to open the Lark Creek Inn—"an American country restaurant" featuring the freshest seasonal ingredients—in a Victorian historical landmark building in Larkspur, Marin County, California. In 1993 he opened One Market Restaurant in downtown San Francisco. Two years later he launched Lark Creek Cafe in Walnut Creek in the East Bay area, followed shortly after by the opening of Lark Creek Cafe in San Mateo. In 1993 Bradley received the James Beard Foundation's award as Best Chef in California, and his first cookbook, *Bradley Ogden's Breakfast, Lunch, and Dinner,* won the prestigious International Association of Culinary Professionals' Award for best cookbook.

Grilled Lumberjack Steaks with Wild Mushroom Sauce and Potato Wedges

SERVES 4

For the Steaks:
1 cup piquant tomato salsa
2 tablespoons olive oil
4 porterhouse steaks, about 16 to 18 ounces each

For the Potato Wedges:
6 large unpeeled baking potatoes, cut in half lengthwise
2 tablespoons peanut or vegetable oil
Salt
Freshly cracked black pepper

For the Wild Mushroom Sauce:
2 cups beef stock (page 186)
½ cup sliced smoked bacon
2 tablespoons butter
1 tablespoon minced garlic
1 cup sliced chanterelles or other wild mushrooms (about 4 ounces)
½ cup scallions cut into 1-inch lengths
1 tablespoon minced fresh marjoram
Dash of Worcestershire sauce

These steaks pay tribute to the mighty pine forests of the Pacific Northwest. You don't need the appetite of a lumberjack to consume these hefty steaks, but after you've enjoyed this meal, you'll probably feel strong enough to pick up an axe and split some logs at least!

The delicate trumpet-shaped orange or yellow chanterelle mushrooms are just one of the many types of wild mushrooms that grow in profusion in the forests of the region, and nowadays they are usually available in markets year-round. If need be, you can use any type of wild mushroom for this recipe or, in a pinch, farmed white mushrooms. The chanterelles make a perfect contrasting match for the robust flavors of the steak. Use your favorite brand of tomato-based piquant salsa for this recipe.

....

Preheat the oven to 350 degrees and prepare the grill. (Or, alternatively, the steaks can be broiled or sautéed in a heavy pan or skillet using 1 tablespoon of hot olive oil or safflower oil; they will take approximately the same time to cook as they will on the grill.)

Place the salsa in a food processor or blender and puree until smooth. With the machine running, add the oil in a slow, steady stream until well blended. The mixture should be thin but not soupy. Transfer the salsa mixture to a large shallow dish and coat both sides of the steaks. Cover with plastic wrap and let sit at room temperature for 1 hour.

Cut the potato halves lengthwise into 3 triangular wedges. Place the wedges in a mixing bowl and toss with the oil, salt, and pepper. Transfer the potatoes to a baking sheet and bake in the oven for 45 minutes to 1 hour, until golden brown and tender.

To prepare the mushroom sauce, heat the stock in a saucepan over medium-high heat and reduce to 1 cup. Place the bacon in a sauté pan and cook over medium heat until almost crisp. Remove the bacon from the pan and drain on paper towels.

Melt the butter in the same sauté pan. Add the garlic and mushrooms to the hot pan and sauté over medium-high heat for about 5 minutes, until the mushrooms are tender and the garlic is lightly golden. Add the scallions and sauté 1 minute longer. Add the reduced stock and bring the mixture to a boil. Stir in the cooked bacon, marjoram, and Worcestershire sauce, and remove from the heat.

Transfer the steaks from the salsa to the hot grill. Grill for 6 to 7 minutes per side for medium-rare or 8 to 9 minutes per side for medium. The steaks should have a caramelized and roasty tomato smell when cooking.

To serve, spoon the liquid from the mushroom sauce onto each serving plate and arrange the vegetables from the sauce on one side of the plate. Place a steak over the sauce, lay the potatoes next to the steak and vegetables, and serve immediately.

Filet Mignon with a Red Wine, Shallot, Bone Marrow, and Cèpe Sauce, and Crispy Potato Cakes with Caviar

By Chef Ken Frank, fenix at the Argyle, Los Angeles, California

SERVES 4

10 beef marrow bones, about
    1 inch each

For the Potato Cake Garnish:
¼ cup crème fraîche
Juice of ¼ lemon
1 heaping teaspoon snipped
    fresh chives
Freshly ground white pepper

For the Potato Cakes:
2 unpeeled russet potatoes,
    about 10 ounces each
½ cup peanut oil
4 ounces sturgeon caviar, for
    garnish

For the Sauce:
4 large fresh cèpe mushrooms or
    8 medium cèpes, brushed
    clean with a dry towel
4 tablespoons butter
Salt
Freshly ground black pepper
2 tablespoons very finely
    minced shallots
⅔ cup good-quality Cabernet
    Sauvignon or red Bordeaux
    wine
¾ cup veal stock (page 187)

For the Steaks:
4 filet mignon steaks, about
    8 ounces each
Salt
Freshly ground black pepper

2 teaspoons fresh chervil leaves,
    for garnish

This recipe is unlike the others in this book in that it is a two-course dish: The potato cakes (one of Ken's signature dishes) should be served as an appetizer before the steak and sauce. The cèpe mushrooms and bone marrow highlight the delicious sauce in this elegant recipe. Cèpes, also known as porcinis, are wild mushrooms; they have a pale brown cap that can measure an inch or two across and up to seven or eight inches long. Just recently I picked about thirty pounds of cèpes with some friends on a hike in the Sangre de Cristo Mountains above Santa Fe, New Mexico. We cooked them right away and enjoyed them for days. In this recipe their meaty texture and pleasant, complex earthy flavors complement the steaks well. Avoid washing cèpes unless they are very dirty, or they will become waterlogged and their texture will be too mushy. Bone marrow is underused in the United States, but it is considered a delicacy in European countries. It can be purchased or ordered at most butchers or supermarkets—and ask your butcher or the store to cut the marrow bones for you. You may want to consider the caviar garnish for the potatoes an optional flourish, but it's a wonderful finishing touch.

•••

Carefully remove the marrow from the bones and place in a bowl. Cover the marrow with generously salted water and let soak overnight in the refrigerator; change the water at least once.

To prepare the potato cake garnish, mix together the crème fraîche, lemon juice, chives, and pepper in a bowl. Let sit for 2 hours at room temperature to allow the crème fraîche to rethicken.

Coarsely grate the unpeeled potatoes and loosely form into patties or cakes about ½ inch thick (the size of a homemade ham burger). Do this immediately so the shredded potato does not oxidize and blacken. Heat ⅛ inch of oil in a heavy sauté pan or skillet over medium heat. When the oil is hot, carefully add the potato cakes with a spatula. Fry for 2 to 2½ minutes per side, or until golden brown. Place a dollop of crème fraîche on top of each potato cake and garnish with a spoonful of caviar before serving.

To prepare the sauce and steaks, preheat the oven to 400 degrees and preheat the grill.

Remove the stems from the cèpes, cut the stems into ¼-inch-thick slices, and reserve. Heat 1 tablespoon of the butter in an ovenproof sauté pan or skillet and sauté the cèpe caps over medium heat for about 1 minute. Turn the caps over, season with salt and pepper, and finish cooking in the oven for 7 to 8 minutes (or, alternatively, finish on the grill). Remove from the oven and set aside.

Heat another 1 tablespoon of the butter in a sauté pan. Add the sliced cèpe stems and sauté over medium-high heat until golden brown. Add the shallots and sauté about 30 seconds longer, or until they are soft. Deglaze the pan with the wine and reduce the liquid until the pan is almost dry. Add the stock and reduce slightly, until the sauce begins to thicken.

Remove the pan from the heat. Drain the soaked marrow and cut into ¼-inch-thick slices. Stir the marrow slices into the sauce and let sit for 1 minute to soften; if necessary, heat the pan slightly but do not let the marrow boil. Slowly whisk in the remaining 2 tablespoons of butter, a little at a time. Adjust the seasonings if necessary and keep the sauce warm.

Season the steaks with salt and pepper. Place the filets on the hot grill and cook for 5 to 6 minutes per side for medium-rare or about 7 minutes for medium, or to the desired degree of doneness.

Place the steaks in the center of each warm serving plate and place 2 large (or 1 medium) cèpes, cap side down, next to the meat. Using a slotted spoon, fill the caps with the sauce. Spoon the remaining sauce over the meat and sprinkle the plates with the chervil.

Ken Frank describes himself as a "California-born French chef." He still loves chiliburgers, but his favorite ingredients are truffles, foie gras, and wild mushrooms. Ken was born in Whittier, California, and fell in love with cooking when his father, a teacher, was awarded a fellowship to teach in France for a year and took his family with him. Later, Ken returned to France to train as a chef's apprentice. Following a series of apprenticeships in California, he became head chef at the acclaimed Los Angeles restaurant La Guillotine in 1977 at the age of twenty-one. Two years later Ken became co-owner of the restaurant La Ruche that reopened in the same space, and it was renamed La Toque. Since closing La Toque in 1994, Ken opened The Foundation Room at the House of Blues in Los Angeles, and the following year opened fenix in the Art Deco–style Argyle Hotel on Sunset Boulevard. *Esquire* magazine named fenix one of the Best New Restaurants in the country in 1995. Ken wrote *Ken Frank's La Toque Cookbook*, published by Simon and Schuster in 1992.

Marinated Filet Mignon Steaks with Artichokes and Rosemary Potato Galette

For the Marinade:
½ cup California dry red wine,
    such as Merlot or Pinot Noir
3 tablespoons red wine vinegar
3 garlic cloves, crushed
½ bunch of fresh thyme sprigs
Pinch of freshly ground black
    pepper

For the Steaks:
4 filet mignon steaks,
    7 or 8 ounces each

For the Potato Galette:
4 Idaho potatoes (about
    2 pounds)
8 tablespoons (1 stick) butter,
    melted and hot
Salt
Freshly ground black pepper
1½ teaspoons minced fresh
    rosemary
1 teaspoon minced fresh thyme

For the Artichokes:
2 tablespoons all-purpose flour
2 cups water
½ teaspoon salt
3 lemons, cut in half
4 large artichokes

Salt
4 sprigs fresh rosemary, for
    garnish

Castroville, just north of Monterey in California, proclaims itself "the artichoke capital of the world," and if you've ever driven along that stretch of the Pacific Coast Highway, you can't help but notice the thistlelike artichoke plants that grow in the surrounding fields as far as the eye can see. Artichokes, with their subtle, nutty flavor, make a delicious meal with the marinated steaks and galette, which is the French word for a savory or sweet cake or tart. Galettes are usually round or flat in shape, and this galette recipe is an impressive way to serve potatoes. Use the same wine to accompany the meal as you use in the marinade.

....

Thoroughly combine all the marinade ingredients in a mixing bowl. Place the steaks in a large dish and add the marinade. Cover the dish with plastic wrap and marinate at room temperature for at least 1 hour, turning the steaks once. Or, alternatively, refrigerate overnight (in which case, bring the steaks to room temperature before grilling).

To prepare the galette, peel the potatoes and finely slice, preferably with a mandolin slicer; do not rinse the potatoes because they need the starch to adhere to one another. Coat the bottom of a 10-inch nonstick sauté pan or skillet with 2 tablespoons of the butter. Arrange one-third of the potatoes in the bottom of the skillet in a spiral pattern, starting in the center and working out, overlapping the slices slightly; the bottom of the skillet should be covered with the potatoes. Season with salt and pepper, and sprinkle with one-third of the rosemary and thyme. Drizzle the potato slices with another 2 tablespoons of butter. Arrange another layer of potatoes in the same way, seasoning with salt, pepper, and another one-third of the rosemary and thyme. Drizzle over 2 tablespoons more of the butter. Repeat this process 1 more time with the remaining galette ingredients.

Prepare the grill (or, alternatively, the steaks can also be broiled).

Cook the potatoes over medium-low heat for 8 to 10 minutes, until the bottom layer begins to turn brown and crisp (use a spatula to check). Transfer the skillet to the middle rack of the broiler and cook 10 to 12 minutes longer, or until the top is golden brown and fork-tender. Cut into portions or wedges just before serving.

While the potatoes are cooking, prepare the artichokes: Place the flour in a saucepan and gradually whisk in the water to form a thin paste. Add the salt and bring to a simmer, whisking if necessary to break any lumps. Squeeze the juice from 2 lemons into the saucepan. Remove the pan from the heat.

Break the stem of each artichoke from the base and rub the bottom of the artichokes with the halves of the remaining lemon to prevent discoloration. Slice off and discard the top one-third of the artichokes and remove the outer leaves to expose the bottoms, rubbing them again with the lemon. Cut off the remaining inner leaves just above the artichoke bottoms. Drop the artichokes into the water mixture and add more water to cover. Bring to a boil, lower the heat, cover the pan, and simmer for 25 to 30 minutes, until the artichokes are tender when pierced with a knife. Drain, scoop out the fuzzy choke with a spoon, and discard. Reheat in hot salted water if necessary just before serving.

Remove the filets from the marinade and pat dry. Season with salt and grill over a medium-hot fire for 5 to 6 minutes per side for medium-rare or about 7 minutes per side for medium.

To serve, place the filets on one side of each warm serving plate and a portion of the potato galette next to the steaks. Serve with the artichokes and garnish the galette with the rosemary.

Parker Ranch Filet Mignon with Pan-Crisped Maui Onions and Honey-Mustard Sauce

By Chef Roy Yamaguchi, Roy's, Honolulu, Hawaii

SERVES 4

For the Honey-Mustard Sauce:

¼ cup peanut oil

2 sweet Maui onions, chopped
   (about 1 cup)

8 garlic cloves, minced

¾ cup chopped carrots

¾ cup chopped celery

4 bay leaves

5 black peppercorns

1 cup port or Cabernet
   Sauvignon wine

4 cups veal stock (page 187)

1 cup whole-grain mustard

⅓ cup honey

10 tablespoons butter, chopped

For the Onions:

1 cup peanut oil

1½ cups all-purpose flour

4 large sweet Maui onions, very
   finely julienned

For the Steaks:

4 filet mignon steaks, about
   8 ounces each

Salt

Freshly ground black pepper

Many people are surprised to learn that the second largest cattle ranch in the United States is located on the big island of Hawaii. It must also be the most scenic, lying beneath the majestic slopes of Mauna Kea, the fourteen-thousand-foot dormant volcano. The ranch was established in the mid-1800s by John Palmer Parker, a former New Englander who received a land grant from the Hawaiian king. Today, the ranch occupies over two hundred thousand acres and has more than fifty thousand head of cattle.

In this recipe Roy matches the beef with a clean-flavored honey-mustard sauce and the local sweet onions from Maui, which are one of the island's major vegetable crops. Other sweet onions, such as Vidalia (from Georgia), Walla Walla (from Washington State), or Texas Noon Day, can be substituted, although Roy will tell you the sweet onions from the islands are "ono"—the best.

....

Prepare the grill (or, alternatively, the steaks can be broiled).

To prepare the sauce, heat the oil in a heavy saucepan. Add the onions, garlic, carrots, celery, bay leaves, and peppercorns to the hot pan and sauté over medium-high heat for about 5 minutes, stirring occasionally until golden brown. Deglaze the pan with the port and add the stock, mustard, and honey. Reduce the liquid to about 2½ cups, stirring constantly until the sauce is thick enough to coat the back of a spoon. Strain through a fine-mesh sieve into a clean saucepan (discard the solids) and return to the heat. Whisk in the butter, a little at a time, and mix thoroughly. Keep the sauce warm over hot water in a double boiler.

To prepare the onions, heat the oil in a deep fryer or heavy saucepan (there should be enough to come at least 1½ inches up the sides of the pan). Place the flour on a plate and lightly dredge the onions in the flour. When the oil is hot, fry the onions for 5 to 7 minutes over medium-high heat, turning constantly but gently, until golden brown. Drain on paper towels, and keep warm.

Season the steaks with salt and pepper. Grill for 5 to 6 minutes per side for medium-rare or about 7 minutes per side for medium.

To serve, place a steak in the center of each warm serving plate and spoon the sauce around the meat. Place a handful of the onions on top of each filet and the rest on the side. Serve immediately.

Roy Yamaguchi was born in Japan, where he attended American schools. As a child he often visited Maui where his grandfather owned a tavern and general store. Roy trained professionally at the Culinary Institute of America and began his career at the Escoffier Room of the Beverly Hills Hilton Hotel. He continued his apprenticeship under Jean Bertranou at L'Ermitage in Los Angeles and at Michael's in Santa Monica. He was executive chef at Le Serene and then Le Gourmet before opening 385 North in Los Angeles in 1984, where he developed his distinctive Euro-Asian cuisine. After four years the restaurant was sold, and Roy moved to Hawaii where he opened Roy's in Honolulu in 1988. Roy's Pacific Rim cuisine has proved such a success that he now owns ten restaurants: five in the Hawaiian Islands, two in Tokyo, and restaurants in Pebble Beach, California, Guam, and Hong Kong. In 1993 Roy was named the Best Chef in the Pacific and Northwest by the James Beard Foundation. Roy's first cookbook, *Roy's Feasts from Hawaii,* was published by Ten Speed Press in 1995.

Pacific Rim Beef Salad with Sesame-Ginger Dressing

SERVES 4

For the Marinade:
2 teaspoons sesame oil
1 teaspoon soy sauce
2 garlic cloves, minced
1 teaspoon freshly cracked black
    pepper
1 teaspoon Chinese plum sauce
1 small serrano chile, seeded
    and minced, or ¼ teaspoon
    cayenne chile powder

For the Steaks:
2 boneless strip sirloin steaks,
    about 10 ounces each

For the Sesame-Ginger Dressing:
½ cup unseasoned rice vinegar
⅓ cup julienned pickled ginger
¼ cup sesame oil
1 tablespoon soy sauce
1 garlic clove, minced

For the Salad:
1 small head Bibb or butter
    lettuce, leaves separated, or
    mizuna lettuce
1 bunch watercress, stemmed
1 red onion, julienned
1 red bell pepper, seeded and
    julienned
1 cup bean sprouts
2 scallions, sliced on a diagonal
1 cucumber, peeled, seeded, and
    sliced on a diagonal

1 tablespoon sesame seeds, for
    garnish

Contemporary Pacific Rim cuisine has become immensely popular on the West Coast and in Hawaii over the last few years, inspired by chefs such as Wolfgang Puck (Chinois-on-Main in Venice, California), Roy Yamaguchi, and Alan Wong in Hawaii, among many others. This cuisine is based on using flavors and ingredients from different Asian countries, such as Japan, China, Thailand, Vietnam, and Indonesia, and combining them in innovative ways, often in a distinctly American context or style. California is, after all, very much a part of the Pacific Rim. This salad, with its delicious Asian nuances, is a fine example of this exciting style of eating. The plum sauce in the marinade (also called duck sauce) is a sweet-and-sour Chinese condiment made with plums and apricots that, like the pickled ginger in the dressing, is available in most supermarket Asian food sections.

• •

Thoroughly combine all the marinade ingredients in a large dish. Turn the steaks in the marinade and cover the dish with plastic wrap. Marinate at room temperature for at least 1 hour, turning the steaks once. Or, alternatively, refrigerate overnight (in which case, bring to room temperature before sautéing).

To prepare the dressing, whisk together all the ingredients in a mixing bowl until emulsified. Set aside.

Remove the steaks from the marinade and pat dry. Heat a dry, heavy sauté pan or skillet and sear the steaks over medium-high heat for about 4 minutes per side, until just medium-rare. Remove the steaks from the pan and let rest.

Toss all the salad ingredients together with the dressing in a large mixing bowl.

Toast the sesame seeds in a dry skillet over medium-high heat for 45 seconds to 1 minute, tossing continuously, until golden brown and shiny.

To serve, cut the steaks into thin slices. Place a mound of tossed salad in the center of each serving plate and top with the steak slices. Sprinkle the toasted sesame seeds on top and serve.

6

Classic
Steak
Recipes

Prime Rib with Blue Cheese Sauce and Garlic Mashed Potatoes

SERVES 4

For the Prime Rib:
3 pounds boneless rib-eye roast,
  trimmed of excess fat
Salt
Freshly ground black pepper

**For the Garlic Mashed
Potatoes:**
2 pounds russet potatoes, peeled
  and chopped
3 garlic cloves, thinly sliced
4 tablespoons butter
½ cup heavy cream
Salt
Freshly ground black pepper

For the Blue Cheese Sauce:
1 tablespoon butter
4 shallots, minced
2 cloves garlic, minced to a
  paste
½ cup white wine
1 cup heavy cream
½ cup crumbled blue cheese,
  such as Maytag, Gorgonzola,
  or Stilton
Dash of Worcestershire sauce
Salt
Freshly ground black pepper

Tender, juicy prime rib (also called rib roast) cut into thick slices gives a steaklike texture and a distinctive flavor that is complemented by the rich and tangy blue cheese sauce and garlicky potatoes. Ask your butcher for the loin end of the rib eye, which has less fat. I recommend using a meat thermometer for cooking the rib-eye roast because it takes a lot of the guesswork out of the doneness of the beef. Many ovens can be as much as 25 to 50 degrees off the correct temperature, so inserting a thermometer in the thickest part of the roast should ensure accurate results. Use your favorite blue cheese in the sauce; the addition of the pan drippings will add a great deal of flavor and help tie the whole dish together deliciously.

· ·

Preheat the oven to 450 degrees.

Season the prime rib on both sides with salt and pepper. Place in a roasting pan and sear in the oven for 15 minutes. Lower the oven temperature to 325 degrees and continue cooking for about 1 hour for rare, or until the meat reaches an internal temperature of 125 degrees; 1¼ hours (or an internal temperature of 130 to 135 degrees) for medium-rare; or about 1 hour and 25 minutes (or an internal temperature of 140 degrees) for medium. Remove the meat from the oven and let rest for about 5 minutes before slicing. Reserve 1 cup of the pan drippings for the blue cheese sauce.

About 30 minutes before the prime rib is ready, prepare the potatoes. Place the potatoes in a large saucepan of salted water and bring to a boil. Cook at a low boil for about 15 minutes, until tender.

Meanwhile, combine the garlic, butter, and cream in a saucepan, and simmer for about 20 minutes. Transfer the mixture to a blender and puree until smooth. Drain the potatoes, place in a mixing bowl, and add the garlic cream puree. Mash

together with a potato masher or fork, leaving them smooth or lumpy, as you prefer. Season with salt and pepper. Cover the bowl with foil to keep warm.

To prepare the sauce, melt the butter in a saucepan. Add the shallots and garlic, and sauté over medium heat for 2 minutes. Deglaze the pan with the wine and bring to a boil. Stir in the 1 cup of reserved meat drippings and return to a boil. Stir in the cream, return to a boil, then lower the heat to a simmer until the sauce thickens. Stir in the blue cheese and Worcestershire sauce, and season with salt and pepper.

To serve, slice the prime rib into 4 thick slices and place each slice in the center of a warm serving plate. Spoon the sauce over the meat, place a mound of the potatoes next to the meat, and serve immediately.

Top Sirloin Steak Sandwiches with Cheese, Tomatoes, and Caramelized Onions

For the Caramelized Onions:
1 tablespoon vegetable oil
1 large white onion, sliced
⅛ teaspoon salt
⅛ teaspoon sugar
⅛ teaspoon ground fennel seeds
1 teaspoon sherry vinegar

For the Steaks:
4 top sirloin steaks, about
    8 ounces each
Salt
Freshly ground black pepper
2 ounces smoked Cheddar,
    smoked Gouda, or Jalapeño
    Jack cheese, thinly cut into
    8 or 12 slices

For the Sandwiches:
2 tablespoons butter, softened
1 tablespoon whole-grain
    mustard
4 Kaiser rolls or French bread
    rolls, cut in half lengthwise
8 romaine lettuce leaves
2 ripe tomatoes, sliced

There are times when you feel like having a sandwich, and nothing less than a thick, juicy steak sandwich will do! Well, this is the recipe for those occasions! I always look forward to the hearty beef flavor and firm texture of top sirloin, and I recommend USDA prime grade and well-trimmed center cuts. Pounding the steaks lightly with a meat mallet or rolling pin not only makes them easier to eat but helps tenderize them.

The technique of slowly caramelizing onions accentuates their natural sweet tones and gives them a depth of flavor. You can use sweet onions (such as Vidalia or Maui) if you want an almost syrupy topping for the steaks.

Use the smaller, more tender inner romaine leaves for the sandwich, and fresh vine-ripened tomatoes if possible. If you like smoky flavors, a good-quality smoked cheese will complement and highlight the grilled flavor of the steaks, especially if you use soaked mesquite or hickory wood chips on the grill.

Prepare the grill. Or, alternatively, the steaks can be broiled or sautéed in a heavy pan or skillet using 1 tablespoon of vegetable oil; they will take approximately the same time to cook as they will on the grill.

To prepare the caramelized onions, heat the oil in a sauté pan or skillet. Add the onion, salt, sugar, and ground fennel, and sauté over medium-high heat for 10 minutes, until the onion turns golden brown. Deglaze the pan with the vinegar, remove the pan from the heat, and let cool.

Pound the steaks lightly with a meat mallet and season on both sides with salt and pepper. Grill for about 4 minutes per side for medium-rare or 5 to 6 minutes per side for medium. Transfer the steaks to a platter and cover with the cheese slices so they melt slightly.

To assemble the sandwiches, mix the butter and mustard together and spread on both sides of the rolls. Toast lightly on the grill or under the broiler, then remove. Place 2 lettuce leaves on the bottom half of each roll and add the tomato slices. Then add the steaks and cover them with the caramelized onions. Add the top half of the rolls and place toothpicks in the sandwiches to hold them together. Cut the sandwiches in half, place on serving plates, and serve with chips or fries if desired.

Wine-Marinated Rib-eye Steaks with Herbed Mustard Sauce and Wilted Spinach

For the Marinade:
1 tablespoon dry mustard
    powder
½ teaspoon minced garlic
Freshly cracked black pepper to
    taste
1 teaspoon Worcestershire sauce
½ cup good-quality dry red wine
½ cup olive oil

For the Steaks:
4 rib-eye steaks, about 10 ounces
    each

For the Mustard Sauce:
2 tablespoons light olive oil
2 garlic cloves, minced
½ white onion, finely diced
1 small carrot, finely diced
½ stalk celery, finely diced
¼ cup white wine vinegar or
    champagne vinegar
2 cups veal stock (page 187)
3 tablespoons Dijon mustard
1 tablespoon wine mustard or
    horseradish mustard
Dash of Worcestershire sauce
Salt
Freshly cracked black pepper
1 teaspoon chopped fresh thyme
1 teaspoon chopped fresh
    tarragon
1 tablespoon butter (optional)

1 tablespoon light olive oil

When selecting rib-eye steaks, ask your butcher for the low side (or loin end) of the rib, which is the section of the rib eye that has no "kernel fat" or muscle separation. When marinating steaks in red wine, it's important not to let them sit for too long. Some people think that the longer you leave the steak in a marinade, the more flavor it absorbs. Beyond a certain point, however, the acid in the wine will "cook" the meat and break down its fibers, giving it a stringier and less smooth texture.

The tasty, spicy mustard sauce is based on a mirepoix, or mixture of sautéed vegetables. The flavor of the sauce echoes that of the marinade, creating a smooth and seamless transition between the meat and the sauce. Using the same wine that you used for the marinade to accompany the meal likewise ties together the major elements of this dish.

....

To prepare the marinade, mix together the mustard, garlic, pepper, and Worcestershire sauce in a mixing bowl. Whisk in the wine until all the ingredients are combined and then whisk in the oil.

Place the steaks in a large dish and pour the marinade over them. Cover the dish with plastic wrap and marinate at room temperature for 1 hour.

To prepare the sauce, heat the oil in a saucepan. Add the garlic, onion, carrot, and celery, and sauté over medium-high heat for about 2 minutes. Deglaze the pan with the vinegar, add the stock, and bring to a boil. Lower the heat to medium-low, add both of the mustards, and simmer gently for about 20 minutes; do not boil, or the mustard will "break." Add the Worcestershire sauce and season with salt and pepper. Strain through a medium-fine sieve into a clean saucepan and keep warm. Just before serving, add the thyme and tarragon, and if you want to give the sauce an attractive sheen, stir in the butter until thoroughly blended.

Remove the steaks from the marinade and wipe off any excess. Heat the olive oil in a heavy sauté pan or skillet and sear the steaks in the hot pan over medium-high heat for 5 to 6 minutes per side for medium-rare or 7 to 8 minutes per side for medium.

Meanwhile, to prepare the spinach, melt the butter in a sauté pan. Add the shallots and sauté over medium heat for about 1 minute. Add the spinach and sauté for about 2 minutes, until lightly wilted.

To serve, ladle the sauce onto warm serving plates. Place the steaks on top of the sauce, put the spinach next to the steaks, and serve immediately.

For the Spinach:
3 tablespoons butter
2 shallots, minced
1 pound spinach, washed and left slightly damp (see page 58)

Steaks Diane with Red Onion Compote

For the Red Onion Compote:
2 red onions, thinly sliced,
    rinsed in cold water and
    drained
¼ cup honey
¼ cup red wine vinegar
¼ cup Cabernet Sauvignon wine
1 sprig fresh rosemary
Pinch of salt

For the Steaks:
4 filet mignon steaks, about
    6 ounces each, pounded
    lightly with a meat pounder,
    meat mallet, or rolling pin to
    a thickness of about ¾ inch
¼ teaspoon salt
Freshly ground black pepper
1 tablespoon Dijon mustard
5 tablespoons butter
2 tablespoons minced shallots
1 tablespoon brandy
Juice of 1 lemon
1 tablespoon Worcestershire
    sauce
1 tablespoon snipped fresh
    chives

This classic recipe is often prepared in restaurants table-side, and although the flaming brandy is certainly an impressive effect, we recommend that you cook this dish in the safety of your kitchen!

To enhance the flavors and textures of the presentation, add some sliced mushrooms to the pan with the shallots after you have removed the steaks. The mustard seasoning gives the filets a kick, and it combines well with the honey in the onion compote to give a delicious sweet-and-hot combination—one that never fails to satisfy. Flattening the steaks a little ensures that they cook through before the seasoning scorches.

The compote will keep well in the refrigerator for at least four or five days. If you want to serve this dish with a starch, a traditional accompaniment is Château potatoes. Peel small new potatoes or cut larger potatoes to the size of big olives, sauté them briefly in butter and then oven-roast them until golden brown.

To prepare the onion compote, combine the onions, honey, vinegar, wine, and rosemary in a saucepan and cook over low heat, stirring occasionally, for 30 minutes, until thickened and syrupy. Remove the rosemary and discard. Season with salt and let cool to room temperature before serving.

Season the steaks with the salt and pepper, and rub evenly with the mustard. Heat 2 tablespoons of the butter in a heavy sauté pan or skillet. Sear the steaks over medium-high heat for 2 to 3 minutes per side for medium-rare or 3 to 4 minutes per side for medium. Remove the steaks and keep warm. Add the shallots to the pan and sauté over medium heat for 1 minute. Deglaze the pan with the brandy; carefully ignite, shake the pan, and turn the heat to medium-low. Stir in the lemon juice, Worcestershire sauce, and the remaining 3 tablespoons of butter until thoroughly incorporated. Stir in the chives and adjust the seasonings as necessary.

To serve, place a steak in the center of each warm serving plate and cover with the sauce. Spoon the onion compote next to the steak and serve immediately.

Filet Mignon Steaks with Merlot Sauce and Wild Mushrooms

For the Merlot Sauce:
3 tablespoons light olive oil
2 garlic cloves, minced
1 onion, diced
1 small carrot, sliced
1 stalk celery, sliced
1 tablespoon tomato paste
2 cups good-quality Merlot wine
3 bay leaves
Pinch of dried thyme
½ teaspoon black peppercorns
3 cups veal stock (page 187)

For the Steaks:
4 filet mignon steaks,
    7 to 8 ounces each
Salt
Freshly ground black pepper
3 tablespoons light olive oil

For the Wild Mushrooms:
2 tablespoons minced shallots
1 pound wild mushrooms, such
    as chanterelles, morels, or
    porcini
2 tablespoons butter
1 tablespoon chopped fresh
    flat-leaf parsley

Two traditional and natural partners of steaks are red wine and wild mushrooms, and this recipe combines them in a succulent way. I like the soft, mellow tones of Merlot, but you can use a more robust, fruity Cabernet Sauvignon, a spicy, complex Pinot Noir, or a peppery Zinfandel if you prefer. Likewise, you can vary the type of mushroom to accompany the steak—it all depends on seasonal availability and your personal preference. A mixture of mushrooms will also work well. The main thing is that their meaty texture and earthy tones complement both the filets and the wine sauce. Serve with Garlic Mashed Potatoes (page 116) or Spicy Mashed Potatoes (page 74) if you wish.

....

To prepare the sauce, heat the oil in a saucepan. Add the garlic, onion, carrot, and celery, and sauté over medium heat for about 7 or 8 minutes, until the onion is lightly browned. Stir in the tomato paste and cook for about 2 minutes. Deglaze the pan with the wine and then stir in the bay leaves, thyme, and peppercorns. Bring the sauce to a boil over medium-high heat and reduce by half. Add the stock and return to a boil. Lower the heat to a simmer and cook the sauce, stirring occasionally, for about 30 minutes, until reduced to about 2 cups of liquid. Strain through a fine-mesh sieve into a clean saucepan and keep warm.

Season the steaks on both sides with salt and pepper. Heat the oil in a sauté pan, add the steaks to the hot pan, and sear over medium-high heat for about 5 to 6 minutes per side for medium-rare or about 7 minutes per side for medium. Remove the steaks from the pan and keep warm.

Add the shallots and mushrooms to the same pan and sauté over medium-high heat for about 5 minutes, until lightly brown.

Add the Merlot sauce and bring to a simmer. Reduce the liquid by half and stir in the butter until thoroughly incorporated. Add the parsley just before serving.

Place the steaks in the center of warm serving plates or shallow serving bowls and spoon the mushrooms and sauce over and around the filets. Serve immediately.

Beef Filets with Asparagus and a Roasted Shallot and Tarragon Sauce

SERVES 4

For the Roasted Shallot and Tarragon Sauce:
1 tablespoon butter, diced
20 large shallots, peeled and
*   with roots slightly attached*
¾ cup heavy cream
2 tablespoons red wine, such as
*   Cabernet Sauvignon or Merlot*
2 teaspoons minced fresh
*   tarragon or ¾ teaspoon dried*
¼ teaspoon salt
⅛ teaspoon freshly ground black
*   pepper*

For the Steaks:
4 filet mignon steaks, about
*   8 ounces each*
1 tablespoon tamari
Freshly ground black pepper
1 tablespoon light olive oil

For the Asparagus:
1 pound fresh asparagus
1 to 2 tablespoons butter, diced
Salt to taste

Tarragon's assertive, fragrantly herbal quality, with hints of anise, brings out the best in beef, and tarragon is the main flavoring in béarnaise sauce (see page 132). Tarragon also complements the dark, rich tamari that is rubbed into the steaks in this recipe. Tamari is a Japanese condiment similar to soy sauce but more mellow-flavored, and it offers a change from using salt to season the steaks.

The peak season for asparagus is March or April through June. Choose tender asparagus spears that are no thicker than a pencil. In those months when asparagus is not in season, serve with steamed broccoli or leeks.

• •

Preheat the oven to 400 degrees.

To prepare the sauce, melt the butter in a sauté pan or skillet. Add the shallots and toss to coat well. Transfer the shallots to a baking dish and roast in the oven for 10 minutes. Remove the baking dish and stir in the cream, wine, tarragon, salt, and pepper. Return to the oven and roast for 30 minutes.

Meanwhile, rub the steaks with the tamari and pepper. Heat the oil in a heavy sauté pan or skillet and sear the steaks for about 5 to 6 minutes per side for medium-rare or about 7 minutes per side for medium.

While the steaks are cooking, prepare the asparagus. Place in a steamer or in a steamer basket set over a saucepan of boiling water. Steam for about 5 minutes, or until tender. Transfer to a serving platter, dot with the butter and let it melt over the asparagus, and season with salt.

To serve, place each steak in the center of a warm serving plate and spoon the sauce around the meat. Place the shallots evenly around the steaks and arrange the asparagus spears artistically around the steaks in spoke fashion or to the side. Serve immediately.

Peppered Steaks Flamed with Brandy

Adapted from a recipe by the late James Beard

SERVES 4

For the Steaks:
*4 boneless strip sirloin steaks,
    about 10 ounces each
1 tablespoon coarsely cracked
    black pepper
Salt
2 tablespoons olive oil*

For the Sauce:
*2 tablespoons olive oil
2 shallots, minced
1 cup sliced mushrooms
¼ cup brandy or Armagnac
1 teaspoon Worcestershire sauce
1 tablespoon chopped fresh
    chives or flat-leaf parsley
    (optional)
4 tablespoons cold butter*

Many years ago I had the pleasure of working with the late James Beard, who taught me much about cooking steaks and other meat. I had approached the "dean of American cookery" and asked him whether he would try some of our Omaha Steaks and write some recipes especially for us. He was really impressed by the steaks and graciously accepted the assignment. Here is one of his recipes, which we have embellished slightly with the addition of the sauce. Peppered steak—steak au poivre—is a traditional recipe that can be made using green or black peppercorns. Both are actually unripe corns; the black are picked green and then dried in the sun and their outer covering left on. You can crush the peppercorns in a mortar with a pestle or with a rolling pin, or whirl them briefly in a blender to give them a coarse texture. If you would like to serve a side dish, prepare the Wilted Spinach (page 120) or steamed asparagus (page 127).

· ·

About 30 minutes before cooking them, press the pepper into both sides of the steaks and season with a little salt. Heat the oil in a heavy-bottomed skillet or sauté pan, add the steaks, and sauté over medium-high heat for about 4 minutes per side for medium-rare and 5 to 6 minutes per side for medium. Remove the meat from the pan and keep warm.

To prepare the sauce, pour off any excess fat from the pan, and heat the oil. Add the shallots and mushrooms, and sauté over medium heat for 2 to 3 minutes. Carefully add the brandy and ignite, letting the alcohol burn off. Stir in the Worcestershire sauce and chives. Stir in the butter, 1 tablespoon at a time, until the sauce is thoroughly combined and smooth.

Place the steaks on warm serving plates, spoon the sauce over them, and serve immediately.

Grilled Porterhouse Steaks with Thyme and Baked Potato Skins

SERVES 4

For the Potato Skins:
2 large russet potatoes
Salt
Freshly ground black pepper
1 tablespoon butter, melted

For the Steaks:
4 porterhouse steaks, about
    16 ounces each
2 tablespoons olive oil
Salt
½ teaspoon cayenne, or to taste
1 tablespoon minced fresh
    thyme

When you're hungry and in the mood for a large, satisfying steak, there's nothing quite like a porterhouse. These steaks were named after the English porter houses (inns and coach houses that served "porter" ale) where travelers in the early 1800s stopped to dine on steak and ale. Porterhouse steaks became popular in the United States around 1814 when a New York City tavern keeper, Martin Morrison, began serving them. Seasoning the steaks with cayenne and thyme gives them a refreshing fragrance and just enough zip to tantalize the taste buds.

The preparation for the potatoes is very simple, and you can grate a little Cheddar or Monterey Jack cheese over them as soon as you take them out of the oven, or you can garnish them with some finely sliced chives. This is a filling dish, but serve it with a vegetable from another recipe in this book if your guests have hearty appetites.

Preheat the oven to 375 degrees and prepare the grill. (Or, alternatively, the steaks can be broiled or sautéed in a heavy pan or skillet using 1 tablespoon of olive oil or safflower oil; they will take approximately the same time to cook as they will on the grill.)

Bake the potatoes in the oven for 1 hour, or until cooked through. Remove from the oven and let cool. Scoop out the flesh of the potatoes and reserve for another use (such as mashed potatoes). Cut the potato skins into wedges, season with salt and pepper, and drizzle with the melted butter. Place the skins on a baking sheet and return to the oven to bake for about 10 minutes, or until crisp and golden brown.

Rub the steaks with the oil and season both sides with the salt and cayenne. Sprinkle with the thyme and press into the meat to coat. Place the steaks on the hot grill and cook for 5 to 6 minutes per side for medium-rare or 7 to 8 minutes for medium.

To serve, place the steaks on warm serving plates with the potato skins next to them. Serve immediately.

7

Steak Recipes
from Europe

Grilled Filet Mignon Steaks with Béarnaise Sauce

SERVES 4

For the Béarnaise Sauce:

2 tablespoons white wine
    vinegar
2 tablespoons dry white wine
2 tablespoons minced shallots
1 tablespoon chopped fresh
    tarragon or 1 teaspoon dried
¼ teaspoon salt
3 egg yolks
8 tablespoons (1 stick) butter,
    melted
Pinch of cayenne, or to taste
½ teaspoon minced fresh
    tarragon or chervil, for
    garnish

For the Filets:

1 tablespoon olive oil
1 teaspoon dry mustard
Salt
Freshly ground black pepper
4 filet mignon steaks, about
    8 ounces each

4 sprigs fresh tarragon, for
    garnish

The origin of béarnaise sauce—a great French classic—is the province of Béarn in southwest France bordering on the Pyrenees Mountains. This is French Basque country where gastronomy is taken seriously. The sauce is said to date from the time of Henry IV in the late sixteenth century. Serve with asparagus, a mixed green salad, or a potato side dish from another recipe. Consider serving this dish with eggs and toasted English muffins or rustic bread for a hearty brunch or breakfast.

• •

Prepare the grill. (Or, alternatively, the steaks can be broiled or sautéed in a heavy pan or skillet using 1 tablespoon of hot olive oil or safflower oil; they will take approximately the same time to cook as they will on the grill.)

To prepare the sauce, combine the vinegar, wine, shallots, tarragon, and salt in a small saucepan and bring to a boil. Lower the heat to a simmer and reduce the liquid by half. Let cool until lukewarm. Transfer to the top of a double boiler and add the egg yolks, whisking in briskly. Add the butter in a slow, steady stream and whisk until the sauce thickens. Season with the cayenne and keep warm. Add a little water if the sauce becomes too thick. Strain into a clean saucepan just before serving, garnished with the minced tarragon.

To prepare the steaks, mix together the oil, mustard, salt, and pepper in a small bowl and rub the mixture on the filets. Grill over a hot flame for 5 to 6 minutes per side for medium-rare or about 7 minutes per side for medium.

To serve, place each steak in the center of a warm serving plate. Spoon the sauce over and around the filets or, alternatively, place in small ramekins or eggcups to the side of the steaks. Garnish the steaks with the tarragon sprigs.

Rib-eye Steaks with Ratatouille and Gratin Potatoes à la Dauphinoise

For the Gratin Potatoes:

1 garlic clove, crushed
3 tablespoons butter
2 cups milk
1 egg
1½ to 2 pounds baking potatoes,
   peeled and thinly sliced
Salt
Freshly ground black pepper
Pinch of nutmeg
1 cup grated Gruyère cheese

For the Ratatouille:

2 tablespoons extra-virgin olive
   oil
1 shallot, minced
2 garlic cloves, minced
1 small red onion, finely diced
2 tablespoons tomato paste
1 small zucchini, diced
1 small red bell pepper, seeded
   and diced
1 eggplant (about 1 pound),
   peeled and diced
1 yellow squash, diced
4 Roma (plum) tomatoes, cored
   and diced
1 cup vegetable or chicken stock
½ tablespoon balsamic vinegar
1 tablespoon minced fresh basil
Salt
Freshly ground black pepper

Ratatouille, the traditional Provençal vegetable stew, is just as delicious served cold as warm. If you use the slender "finger" Japanese eggplants rather than the rounder Italian eggplant, there is no need to peel them. To simplify this recipe, substitute a side salad for the ratatouille or serve grilled or sautéed eggplant.

Gratin refers to a thin crust (usually browned) that forms on the surface of a dish because it is cooked in the oven or under a broiler. This technique is a hallmark of the Dauphiné region of France, which stretches from the Alps to the Rhône Valley—hence the name of this particular preparation for the potatoes in this recipe, "à la Dauphinoise."

···

Preheat the oven to 400 degrees.

To prepare the potatoes, rub a baking dish with the garlic, discard the garlic, and then rub the dish generously with 1 tablespoon of the butter.

Heat the milk in a saucepan to just below a boil. Place the egg in a mixing bowl and very slowly stir in the hot milk to temper. Set aside.

Place the potatoes in a separate mixing bowl and toss with the salt, pepper, and nutmeg. Arrange a layer of the potato slices on the bottom of the dish, barely cover with some of the milk mixture, and sprinkle with a layer of the cheese. Repeat this process until all the ingredients have been layered, ending with a layer of cheese on top. Dice the remaining 2 tablespoons of butter and sprinkle all over the top of the baking dish.

Bake the potatoes in the oven for 45 minutes, until tender and browned on the top. If the potatoes brown too quickly, cover with aluminum foil. Remove from the oven and let rest for 5 minutes before cutting or spooning out.

Prepare the grill. (Or, alternatively, the steaks can be broiled or sautéed in a heavy pan or skillet using 1 tablespoon of olive oil or safflower oil; they will take approximately the same time to cook as they will on the grill.)

To prepare the ratatouille, heat the oil in a sauté pan. Add the shallot, garlic, and red onion, and sauté over medium-high heat for 1 minute. Stir in the tomato paste and cook 30 seconds longer. Add the zucchini, bell pepper, eggplant, yellow squash, and tomatoes, and stir for 1 minute. Add the stock and simmer for about 5 minutes, until the vegetables are tender and most of the liquid has evaporated. Stir in the vinegar and basil, and season with salt and pepper. The ratatouille should have a stewlike consistency; if it seems dry, add a little more stock or water. Keep warm over very low heat.

Season the steaks with salt and pepper, and press the herbs onto both sides of the meat. Place on the grill and cook for about 5 minutes per side for medium-rare or 6 to 7 minutes per side for medium.

To serve, place the steaks in the center of warm serving plates. Spoon the ratatouille on one side of the steaks and the potatoes on the other. Serve immediately.

For the Steaks:
4 rib-eye steaks, about 10 ounces each
Salt
Freshly ground black pepper
1 teaspoon dried herbes de Provence or mixed dried herbs

Entrecôte Steaks with Bordelaise Sauce and Galette Potatoes

Potato Galette (page 108)
4 ounces beef marrow, cut into
    ¼-inch slices

For the Steaks:
4 boneless strip steaks, about
    10 ounces each
Salt
Freshly ground black pepper
2 tablespoons clarified butter

For the Bordelaise Sauce:
3 cups veal stock (page 187)
2 tablespoons minced shallots
1 cup dry red wine, preferably
    from Bordeaux
2 tablespoons butter
Freshly ground black pepper

Entrecôte literally means "between the ribs" in French, and the term refers to the particularly tender cut of steak between the ninth and eleventh ribs. Styles of steaks and beef cuts change over time and from country to country, but from my experience the classic French entrecôte steaks are usually what we in the United States refer to as boneless strip loin roast or boneless strip steaks.

The sauce, named for the Bordeaux region of France from which it originates, is an intense reduction of red wine and veal stock, with the addition of succulent rich beef marrow. For the sauce use the finest Bordeaux wine that your pocketbook will allow and enjoy the remainder with your meal. You won't regret it! Some versions of the sauce include garlic, bay leaves, and a sprig of thyme that are strained off at the end, but using a good-quality wine and stock is sufficient to give this dish plenty of flavor and character.

If you prefer, you can pair this dish with traditional side dishes of seasonal wild mushrooms, such as porcini, or green beans rather than potatoes.

· ·

Prepare the potato galette and keep warm.

Place the marrow in a bowl, cover with generously salted water, and let soak for at least 3 or 4 hours, and preferably overnight, changing the water at least once.

Season the steaks with salt and pepper. Heat the butter in a sauté pan and sauté the steaks over medium-high heat for about 4 minutes per side for medium-rare or 5 to 6 minutes per side for medium. Keep warm.

To prepare the sauce, bring the stock to a boil in a saucepan and reduce by half over medium-high heat. Meanwhile, bring a separate saucepan of salted water to a boil, add the marrow slices, and poach for 3 minutes. Let cool slightly and then dice.

Add the shallots to the same pan used to cook the steaks and sauté over medium-high heat for 1 minute. Deglaze the pan with the wine and reduce by half. Add the reduced stock and bring to a simmer. Reduce the mixture by half again, or until about 1 cup remains. Stir in the butter until thoroughly blended and add the marrow and pepper.

To serve, thinly slice the steaks on a diagonal and fan out the slices in the center of warm serving plates. Place the potatoes next to the steaks, spoon the sauce over the steaks, and serve immediately.

Escoffier's Filets of Beef Chasseur (Hunter Style) with Noisette Potatoes

SERVES 4

For the Noisette Potatoes:
6 russet potatoes
2 tablespoons clarified butter
Salt
Freshly ground black pepper
1 teaspoon minced fresh flat-leaf
  parsley, for garnish

For the Steaks:
4 filet mignon steaks, about
  6 ounces each
Salt
¼ teaspoon cayenne
1 tablespoon olive oil

For the Sauce:
1½ tablespoons olive oil
1 tablespoon minced shallot
1 teaspoon minced garlic
1 pound mushrooms, stemmed
  and sliced
1 tomato, cored and diced
2 tablespoons dry white wine
1 tablespoon brandy
¾ cup veal stock (page 187)
2 tablespoons butter
1 teaspoon chopped fresh thyme
1 teaspoon chopped fresh
  flat-leaf parsley

Auguste Escoffier was one of the greatest chefs who ever lived and one of the most respected and celebrated of the last hundred years or so. Known simply as "The Master" and "The King of Chefs and Chef of Kings," Escoffier was born in southern France in 1847 and spent the last thirty years of his brilliant career in England at the Savoy and then the London Carlton Hotel before retiring in 1921. One of Escoffier's great and lasting legacies was his collection and codifying of traditional and classic French recipes and cooking techniques. He was a born teacher, and through his writings and books, including *Guide Culinaire* and *Ma Cuisine,* he was one of the first chefs to place French haute cuisine within the reach of the home cook. This is one of his steak recipes and one of my favorites.

• •

Preheat the oven to 400 degrees.

To prepare the potatoes, use a Parisian scoop or melon baller to scoop out at least 24 nut-size balls of potato flesh. Heat the butter in an ovenproof pan or skillet and sauté the potato balls over medium heat for 3 to 4 minutes, stirring often. Transfer to the oven and roast for 20 to 30 minutes, stirring occasionally, until tender and golden brown all over. Season with salt and pepper, and keep warm in the oven. Sprinkle with the parsley just before serving.

To cook the steaks, season the filets with salt and cayenne. Heat the oil in a heavy sauté pan or skillet and sear the steaks over medium-high heat for 4 to 5 minutes per side for medium-rare or 6 to 7 minutes per side for medium.

While the steaks are cooking, prepare the sauce. Heat the oil in the same pan used to cook the steaks. Add the shallot and garlic, and sauté over medium-high heat for 1 minute. Add the mushrooms and sauté, while stirring, for 3 minutes. Add the tomato and toss to just heat through. Deglaze the pan with the wine and

brandy, add the stock, and bring to a boil. Lower the heat and simmer for 2 to 3 minutes. Stir in the butter until thoroughly incorporated and stir in the thyme and parsley.

To serve, place the steaks in the center of warm serving plates and spoon the sauce over and around the filets. Decoratively arrange 6 noisette potatoes around each steak and serve immediately.

Beef Stroganoff

By Chef Arturo Valenzuela, The Omaha Club, Omaha, Nebraska

SERVES 4

For the Stroganoff:
4 tablespoons butter
1 pound lean beef tenderloin or
    top sirloin, cut into strips
Salt and freshly ground black
    pepper
½ onion, thinly sliced
¼ cup sliced shiitake mushrooms
¼ cup sliced portobello
    mushrooms
¼ cup sliced chanterelle
    mushrooms
1 tablespoon all-purpose flour
½ cup beef stock (page 186)
½ cup red wine, preferably
    Burgundy or Pinot Noir
1 tablespoon Dijon mustard
¼ cup sour cream

For the Noodles:
1 pound egg noodles
1 tablespoon butter

For the Garnish:
1 ounce enoki mushrooms or
    sliced shiitake mushrooms
1 bunch scallions, sliced on a
    diagonal

This classic beef dish is named after Count Stroganoff, a nineteenth-century Russian diplomat and scion of a wealthy family that owned vast tracts of land and salt refineries in the Urals and later led the conquest of Siberia. It was Count Stroganoff who popularized the family dish in the rest of Europe. You can use top sirloin or tenderloin tips instead of beef tenderloin, and farm-raised mushrooms instead of the wild mushrooms called for in the recipe; in a pinch, use them instead of all the other types, but using several varieties of mushrooms adds to the interesting complexity of flavors in the dish.

· ·

Bring a large saucepan of salted water to a boil.

Heat 2 tablespoons of the butter in a heavy sauté pan or skillet. Season the meat with salt and pepper, add to the pan, and brown on all sides over medium-high heat. Add the onion and mushrooms, and sauté 3 to 4 minutes longer. Cover to keep warm and set aside.

In a separate pan, blend the remaining 2 tablespoons of butter with the flour over low heat to make a roux. When the mixture begins to bubble, gradually stir in the stock and wine. Raise the heat to medium and bring to a boil, while stirring, making sure the mixture is smooth. Stir in the mustard, sour cream, and reserved beef and mushroom mixture, and keep warm.

Meanwhile, add the noodles to the pan of boiling water and cook at a low boil until al dente, about 8 to 10 minutes. Drain, then toss the noodles with the butter to coat.

To serve, arrange the buttered noodles on warm serving plates and top with the stroganoff. Garnish with the mushrooms and scallions, and serve immediately.

Arturo Valenzuela has been devoted to the pleasure of cooking since he began training as a teenager. After four years of apprenticeship under the direction of Walter Hecht, then executive chef of The Omaha Club, Arturo received a diploma in culinary arts. When Hecht, who specializes in German and Swiss cookery, left The Omaha Club to open the Black Bear in downtown Omaha, Arturo cooked and assisted in the management of the kitchen for several years. Arturo spent time learning other parts of the business as a caterer and then helped open the new Marriott Hotel in Omaha before moving to the Marriott in El Paso, Texas. In 1984 he returned to The Omaha Club and shortly there-after was appointed executive chef. Over the years he has developed a wide repertoire of international recipes from many traditional cuisines. He has been especially influenced by produce of the heart-land and the availability of wonderful midwestern beef, which he features in his recipes and menus. For the past three years Arturo has been president of the American Culinary Federation of Omaha.

Tournedos Rossini

3 cups veal stock (page 187)
1 tablespoon clarified butter
1 tablespoon light olive oil
8 tournedos, about ¾ inch to
     1 inch thick and 3 ounces
     each; or 4 filet mignons,
     6 ounces each, cut in half
     crosswise to form medallions
Salt
Freshly ground black pepper
½ cup Madeira wine
2 tablespoons butter
8 slices French bread, lightly
     toasted
8 ounces canned foie gras, cut
     into 8 slices
2 ounces truffles, thinly sliced or
     minced
4 sprigs fresh watercress, for
     garnish

Known for his sensuous and brilliant music, Gioacchino Rossini was the Italian nineteenth-century composer famous for *The Barber of Seville* and *Cinderella,* two of my favorite comic operas. Rossini composed thirty-nine operas in nineteen years and retired at the age of thirty-eight as the most influential opera composer of his time. He was also a renowned gourmet, and his passion for such luxury foods as foie gras and truffles was immortalized by this dish (an egg dish containing these ingredients was also named after Rossini). Make this dish when you want to truly splurge or to deeply impress. Foie gras—goose or duck liver—is thought of as quintessentially French, but it was enjoyed in Egyptian times and introduced to France by the Romans. Truffles, the delicately perfumed underground fungus, is still harvested in the traditional way by using trained pigs and dogs to locate them. This dish is so rich that a side is almost superfluous; however, if you like, serve with Wilted Spinach (page 120) or Noisette Potatoes (page 138).

Preheat the broiler.

In a saucepan, reduce the stock over medium-high heat until 1 cup remains.

Meanwhile, heat the clarified butter and oil in a heavy pan or skillet. Season the tournedos with salt and pepper and sauté over medium-high heat for about 2 to 3 minutes per side until just medium-rare or about 4 minutes per side until just medium.

Remove the tournedos from the pan and pour off the excess fat. Deglaze the pan with the Madeira and add the reduced stock. Bring to a simmer and reduce by about one-quarter, until the sauce thickens slightly. Add the butter to the sauce and stir until thoroughly incorporated.

Place the steaks on top of the toasted bread and top with a slice of foie gras. Place the truffle on top of the foie gras and heat under the broiler for about 1 minute.

Transfer the steaks to warm serving plates and pour the sauce around the tournedos. Garnish with watercress and serve immediately.

Mediterranean Steaks Mirabeaux with Anchovies, Olives, and Couscous

SERVES 4

For the Couscous:
1½ cups water
Pinch of salt
1 teaspoon olive oil
1 cup medium-grain instant
    couscous
2 tablespoons minced fresh
    flat-leaf parsley

For the Steaks:
4 boneless strip steaks, about
    10 ounces each
Salt
Pinch of cayenne

For the Steak Garnish:
20 canned anchovy filets packed
    in oil
10 pimento-stuffed green olives
12 pitted black olives, preferably
    Kalamata (optional)
8 sprigs fresh watercress
    (optional)

This is an eye-catching steak because of the colorful criss-cross pattern that the anchovies and olives make on top of the steak. These two ingredients (with the addition of tomatoes and garlic) are the hallmarks of dishes prepared "à la Niçoise," or in the style of Nice. The delicate granular couscous, which is made from semolina, fits well into the Mediterranean theme, since it is North African in origin and widely eaten as a staple starch in Morocco, Algeria, and Tunisia. Serve this dish with a seasonal green salad if you wish.

• •

Prepare the grill. Or, alternatively, the steaks can be broiled or sautéed in a heavy pan or skillet using 1 tablespoon of hot olive oil or safflower oil; they will take approximately the same time to cook as they will on the grill.

To prepare the couscous, place the water and salt in a saucepan and bring to a boil. Add the oil and couscous, stir once, and remove the pan from the heat. Cover the pan with a lid and let stand for 10 minutes to allow the couscous to absorb the liquid. Fluff the couscous with a fork just before serving and stir in the parsley.

Meanwhile, season the steaks with salt and cayenne. Grill for 4 to 5 minutes per side for medium-rare or about 6 minutes per side for medium.

To serve, place the steaks on warm serving plates. Using 5 anchovies per serving, form into a latticelike or crisscross pattern on top of each steak. Cut each pimento-stuffed olive into 4 slices and arrange 10 slices per serving inside each space created by the latticed anchovies. Serve the couscous next to the steaks and garnish each serving with 3 black olives and 2 watercress sprigs if desired.

Filetto al Carpaccio with an Arugula Salad, Shallot-Dijon Vinaigrette, and Gaufrette Potato Chips

By Chef Alison Barshak, Philadelphia, Pennsylvania

SERVES 4

For the Carpaccio:
8 ounces beef tenderloin, fully trimmed of all fat and silverskin

For the Shallot-Dijon Vinaigrette:
2 tablespoons Dijon mustard
2 tablespoons red wine vinegar
½ cup extra-virgin olive oil
2 tablespoons minced shallots
Salt
Freshly ground black pepper

For the Gaufrette Potato Chips:
1 large russet potato, peeled
3 to 4 cups peanut oil
Salt
Freshly ground black pepper

For the Salad:
Juice of 1 lemon
3 tablespoons olive oil
4 ounces arugula

For the Garnish:
20 large pickled caper berries, stems on, rinsed
6 ounces Parmesan cheese, shaved into long, thin slices
Freshly cracked black pepper

This recipe is Italy's answer to steak tartare, and it makes an impressive appetizer. Carpaccio is made with very thin slices of raw beef tenderloin, so it is important that the meat be very fresh and of particularly high quality. In fact, unless you can guarantee these characteristics, do not attempt this recipe. Freezing the beef tenderloin beforehand makes it a lot easier to cut into paper-thin slices, and it also helps to use a very sharp knife. Prepare the carpaccio immediately before serving it, or it will dry out and lose its distinctive ruby color. The peppery arugula and the crisp potato chips provide interesting counterpoints of flavor and texture to the beef. To make the distinctively patterned potato chips, you will need a mandolin, the French slicer. Alternatively, you can use an inexpensive Japanese slicer, although you will not achieve the same attractive pattern.

• •

Wrap the tenderloin in plastic wrap and freeze for about 1½ hours.

To prepare the vinaigrette, whisk together the mustard and vinegar in a mixing bowl. Slowly whisk in the oil in a steady stream until emulsified. Whisk in the shallots, salt, and pepper until well combined. If the vinaigrette is too thick, whisk in a little water. Set aside.

Remove the tenderloin from the freezer, unwrap, and cut into 4 thin slices. Place each slice on a serving plate, cover with plastic wrap, and lightly pound out as thin as possible with a flat-sided meat mallet or with the flat bottom of a thick, heavy water glass. Flatten so that the beef covers as much of the plate as possible. Keep chilled.

To prepare the potato chips, thinly slice the potatoes with a mandolin, fitted with the crinkle-cut blade on the thin setting. Make one slice across the potato, holding it at a 2 o'clock position and cutting on a diagonal. Turn the potato to a 10 o'clock position and slice again on the opposite diagonal. Adjust the thickness of the blade so that the potatoes have a grid or criss-cross pattern. Place the potatoes in a strainer and rinse under cold running water until the water runs clear.

Heat the oil in a deep fryer or saucepan to 350 degrees (the oil should be 2 to 3 inches deep). Carefully slide the potatoes into the hot oil and fry, turning with tongs, for 1 or 2 minutes, until golden brown. Remove the chips with tongs or a slotted spoon and drain on paper towels. Season with salt and pepper.

To prepare the salad, whisk together the lemon juice and oil in a mixing bowl. Add the arugula and toss together.

Place a small mound of the arugula in the center of each carpaccio and top with the potato chips. Evenly space 5 caper berries around the edge of the salad and arrange the slices of cheese between the caper berries. Drizzle about 1½ tablespoons of the vinaigrette over each serving of carpaccio. Sprinkle the cracked pepper over the whole dish and serve immediately.

Alison Barshak is a nationally acclaimed chef with an innovative approach to Mediterranean cuisine. Born and raised in Philadelphia, Alison was named one of America's Rising Star Chefs by *Restaurant Hospitality* magazine. She is largely self-taught, drawing on more than fifteen years of working in Philadelphia kitchens and her extensive travels. She was appointed head chef at Apropos, a popular and lauded brasserie, before moving to the Central Bar and Grille. Then in 1994, Alison was recruited to open Striped Bass in Philadelphia as executive chef. Striped Bass was the only restaurant in the country serving seafood exclusively, and *Esquire* magazine named it Best New Restaurant of the Year for 1994. Alison is currently working on her first cookbook, and she will be opening her own restaurant in downtown Philadelphia during 1997.

Minute Steaks Dijonaise with Pommes Frites

SERVES 4

For the Pommes Frites:
1 quart vegetable oil
1 pound russet potatoes, cut into
 ⅛-inch shoestring julienne
Salt
Freshly ground black pepper

For the Steaks:
4 top sirloin steaks, about
 6 ounces each, pounded until
 ¼ inch thick
2 tablespoons Dijon mustard
Salt
Freshly ground black pepper
2 tablespoons light olive oil

For the Sauce:
2 tablespoons minced shallots
2 tablespoons dry white wine
¼ cup heavy cream
2 tablespoons butter
1 tablespoon chopped fresh
 flat-leaf parsley

Cooking these steaks "in the Dijon style" involves, as you might expect, the ingredient for which the French city is world-famous: sharp, clean-flavored pale yellow mustard. If you visit Dijon, on the edge of the wine-growing Burgundy region, a walk down the main street will take you past several storefronts with all kinds of mustard pots—and mustards—on display. The city has been a center of mustard making since at least the thirteenth century, and there is no better pairing with mustard than beef. "Pommes frites" is simply the French term for fried potatoes—or, as we call them, French fries; "pommes" is the diminutive form of the French "pommes de terres," or potatoes.

• •

To prepare the potatoes, heat the oil in a deep fryer or large saucepan to 350 degrees.

Rinse the julienned potatoes until the water runs clear; removing the starch this way will ensure that the fries cook crisply. Pat the julienned potatoes dry, carefully add to the hot oil, and fry for 2 to 3 minutes, or until golden brown. Remove the potatoes with a slotted spoon and drain on paper towels. Season with salt and pepper, and keep warm in a low oven.

Rub both sides of the steaks with the mustard and season with salt and pepper. Heat the oil in a heavy sauté pan or skillet. Sauté the steaks over medium-high heat for about 2 minutes on each side for medium-rare or 3 to 4 minutes per side for medium. Remove the steaks from the pan and keep warm in the oven.

To prepare the sauce, add the shallots to the same pan used to cook the steaks and sauté over medium-high heat for 1 minute. Deglaze the pan with the wine, add the cream, and heat through. Stir in the butter until thoroughly incorporated and add the parsley.

To serve, place the steaks in the center of warm serving plates. Spoon the sauce over and around the steaks, place a mound of the potatoes next to the steaks, and serve immediately.

8

Steak Recipes
from Asia

Japanese Beef Teriyaki with Sticky Rice

SERVES 4

For the Marinade:
1 tablespoon finely minced
    ginger
2 garlic cloves, finely minced
1 scallion, finely sliced
1 tablespoon light brown sugar
½ teaspoon crushed red pepper
½ cup soy sauce
2 tablespoons sake or dry sherry

For the Steaks:
4 filet mignon steaks, about
    6 ounces each

For the Rice:
2 cups short-grain white rice

Teriyaki is a Japanese technique of marinating meat (usually beef, pork, or chicken) in a soy sauce–based seasoned marinade before frying, grilling, or broiling it at high temperature. Teriyaki is also the name given to condiment sauces likely to be found on supermarket shelves containing similar ingredients. The sugar in this marinade gives the steak a sweet and glossy glaze, but take care when grilling that the flame does not burn it and make it bitter-tasting. You can double the marinade recipe and reserve half as a dipping sauce for the beef. Of course, in Japan you might find teriyaki made with Kobe beef, an exclusive, full-flavored, and very tender variety that is fed liberal amounts of beer and massaged with sake (sounds like quite a life, doesn't it!). However, you may need to take out a mortgage to try it, since this life of luxury makes Kobe beef extremely expensive at upwards of $100 per pound!

. . . .

Combine all the marinade ingredients in a shallow dish or bowl. Add the steaks and massage with the marinade. Let sit at room temperature for 1 or 2 hours, or refrigerate overnight. Turn the steaks occasionally.

Rinse the rice in a strainer under cold running water until the water no longer looks milky. Soak in a bowl of water for 1 hour.

Prepare the grill (or, alternatively, the steaks can be broiled).

Drain the rice and place in a saucepan with 2 cups of cold water. Bring to a boil, turn the heat to low, and cover the pan with a tight-fitting lid. Simmer for about 15 minutes, or until the water has been absorbed and the rice is sticky and soft. Keep warm.

Remove the steaks from the marinade. Grill for about 4 minutes per side for medium-rare or 5 to 6 minutes per side for medium. Thinly slice across the grain and serve with the rice.

Korean Barbecued Steak with Sticky Rice and Kim Chee

SERVES 4

For the Marinade:
2 tablespoons sesame seeds
¼ cup tamari or soy sauce
2 tablespoons light brown sugar
1 tablespoon unseasoned rice
    vinegar
2 tablespoons dark sesame oil
3 scallions, finely sliced
4 cloves garlic, minced
½ teaspoon minced ginger
1 tablespoon hot chile paste,
    such as sambal sekera or
    Lingham's sauce

For the Beef:
1½ pounds top sirloin, cut into
    ½ inch slices about 3 inches
    long

Sticky Rice (page 153)

For the Garnish:
1 cup kim chee
1 cup bean sprouts
2 serrano chiles, seeded and
    minced
2 tablespoons pickled ginger
12 to 16 large lettuce leaves

Beef is the most popular meat in Korea, and barbecuing it to make dishes such as bulgogi or bulgalbi is a culinary tradition. Sticky short-grain rice is served with every meal. The other ever-present Korean staple is kim chee, the spicy, pungent condiment made from fermented cabbage, radish (daikon), or turnips. Kim chee is available from any Korean grocery store or Asian market. The marinade contains all the key flavors of Korean cuisine, so this is truly a representative dish. The brown sugar in the marinade will give the sliced steak a crispy crust when grilled over high heat, but take care not to let the grill flame up or it will burn the caramelized crust. If you prefer, you can broil the marinated skewers, or you can eliminate the skewers altogether and stir-fry the marinated beef in a wok, using ¼ cup of hot peanut oil.

To prepare the marinade, place the sesame seeds in a dry skillet and toast over medium-high heat, tossing continuously, for about 45 seconds to 1 minute, until golden brown and shiny. Place 1 tablespoon in a mixing bowl and reserve the rest. Add the remaining marinade ingredients to the bowl, stirring until thoroughly combined. Add the sirloin slices and let marinate at room temperature for 2 to 3 hours or in the refrigerator overnight (if refrigerating, bring to room temperature before cooking).

Prepare the rice.

Prepare the grill and soak 20 to 24 wooden skewers in water to prevent them from burning up on the grill (or use metal skewers).

While the rice is cooking, remove the sirloin strips from the marinade and thread each slice onto a separate skewer, pulling them down so they lie flat. Rub the grill with a little sesame oil before cooking to ensure that the meat does not stick to the grill rack. Add the skewers and grill for 1 to 2 minutes per side so they are cooked on the outside but still rare or medium-rare inside.

To serve, spoon a bed of rice on each warm serving plate and top with the skewers. Sprinkle the reserved tablespoon of sesame seeds over the skewers and serve with the garnish ingredients in little bowls for the table to share. If your guests wish, they may place a little of everything inside a lettuce leaf and roll it up, like a tortilla, and eat it with their hands.

Kerala Pineapple Beef Curry with Cucumber Raita

For the Raita:
1 cup plain yogurt
½ English or hothouse cucumber, grated
Pinch of salt
1 teaspoon freshly ground black pepper
Pinch of ground coriander seeds (optional)
1 or 2 sprigs fresh cilantro, for garnish

For the Rice:
2 cups basmati white rice or long-grain American rice
½ teaspoon salt
1 teaspoon lemon juice (optional)

Kerala is the southwesternmost state of India, and the cuisine is marked by two characteristics: spicy foods and ingredients that reflect the region's subtropical location, such as the coconut and pineapple in this sweet curry. This dish cooks quickly, partly because of the tender cut of beef. This is unlike many Indian curries, which need slow, lengthy cooking for all the flavors to fully marry. Curry powder is usually a mixture of fifteen to twenty different ground spices, and Madras curry is a hot variety; use a mild curry powder if you have a low tolerance for spicy food.

In Hindi, "basmati" means "queen of fragrance," and this aromatic rice is higher in quality, more fine textured, and less starchy than other long-grain rice. A fine domestic substitute is Texmati rice, which, as the name suggests, is a type of basmati grown commercially in Texas. Texmati rice can be found in gourmet, specialty, and natural food stores.

The cucumber raita gives a cooling contrast to the curry— it's considerably tastier and more discreet than a small fire extinguisher—so when next in Kerala, just ask for "kakri raita."

• •

To prepare the raita, place the yogurt in a mixing bowl and add the grated cucumber, salt, pepper, and coriander. Mix well and chill in the refrigerator. Garnish with the cilantro just before serving.

Soak the rice in cold water for 10 minutes. Using a strainer, drain the rice and rinse under cold running water until the water no longer looks milky. Place the rice in a saucepan with 4 cups of cold water, the salt, and lemon juice; bring to a boil. Lower the heat to a simmer, stir briefly, and partially cover the pan. Cook for 6 to 8 minutes, or until the water is absorbed; do not stir the rice while it is cooking. Keep warm and fluff with a fork just before serving.

For the Curry:

¼ cup light olive oil
1 pound top sirloin steak, cubed
½ teaspoon salt
1 small white onion, diced
2 tablespoons minced garlic
2 tablespoons minced ginger
2 tablespoons Madras curry
    powder (preferably Patak's or
    Sharwood's), or more to taste
¾ cup frozen pineapple juice
    concentrate, thawed, or
    1½ cups canned pineapple
    juice reduced over high heat
    to ¾ cup
1 small pineapple, peeled,
    cored, and diced
¾ cup beef stock (page 186)
½ cup unsweetened coconut milk

For the Garnish:

¼ cup toasted slivered almonds
12 to 16 fresh cilantro leaves
½ cup mango or other fruit
    chutney

While the rice is soaking and cooking, prepare the curry. Heat the oil in a saucepan or deep, heavy skillet. Season the cubed sirloin with salt, add to the pan, and stir for 5 minutes over medium-high heat, until browned on all sides. Add the onion, garlic, and ginger, and sauté for 1 minute. Stir in the curry powder so that it thoroughly coats all the ingredients and smells toasty and aromatic; sauté for 1 to 2 minutes. Add the pineapple juice concentrate, pineapple, stock, and coconut milk, and bring to a boil. Lower the heat to medium and simmer for 5 minutes so that the liquid reduces slightly. Adjust the seasonings and keep warm.

To serve, place a mound of rice on each warm serving plate and spoon the curry next to or over it. Garnish the curry with the almonds and cilantro, and serve the chutney and raita in bowls on the side.

Korma Gosht (Beef Curry) with Basmati Rice

SERVES 4

For the Curry:
2 tablespoons vegetable oil
1 onion, diced
4 garlic cloves, minced
1 tablespoon minced ginger
10 black peppercorns
2 bay leaves
8 cloves
Pinch of nutmeg
1 cinnamon stick
5 small cardamom pods
2 tablespoons ground almonds
1 pound top sirloin, cubed
1 teaspoon pure red chile
    powder or cayenne
½ teaspoon ground turmeric
1 teaspoon ground fennel seeds
2 teaspoons ground cumin
2 teaspoons ground coriander
    seeds
½ teaspoon salt
½ cup plain yogurt

Basmati Rice (page 156)
Cucumber Raita (page 156)
4 sprigs fresh cilantro, for
    garnish
½ cup mango or other fruit
    chutney

The foods of northern India and Pakistan are broadly similar because Pakistan was created out of the northwestern part of India in 1948, at the time that India achieved independence from Britain. India and Pakistan have coexisted uneasily ever since, though food is one aspect of their culture that the two countries share. In this traditional preparation, the recipe calls for combining your own spices to create a curry.

• •

To prepare the curry, heat the oil in a large saucepan and sauté the onion and garlic over medium-high heat for about 5 minutes, until light brown. Lower the heat to medium and add the ginger, peppercorns, bay leaves, cloves, nutmeg, cinnamon, cardamom, and almonds, and continue to sauté for 1 minute. Add the cubed sirloin, chile powder, turmeric, fennel, cumin, coriander, and salt, and sauté, while stirring, for 5 or 6 minutes, until the mixture is dry. Turn the heat to medium-low, stir in the yogurt, and sauté gently until the mixture becomes dry again. Add 1 cup of water, cover the pan, and cook over low heat for 30 to 35 minutes, or until the meat is tender.

While the curry is cooking, prepare the rice and raita.

To serve, place a mound of rice on each warm serving plate and spoon the curry next to or over it. Garnish the curry with a cilantro sprig. Serve the raita and chutney in bowls on the side.

Beef Filets in Black Bean Sauce with Rice

SERVES 4

For the Steaks:
2 tablespoons soy sauce
1 tablespoon chile oil or
   1 tablespoon peanut oil
   mixed with 1 teaspoon pure
   red chile powder
4 filet mignon steaks, about
   6 ounces each

White Rice (page 162)

For the Black Bean Sauce:
2 tablespoons peanut oil
1 teaspoon minced garlic
1 tablespoon minced ginger
1 red bell pepper, seeded and
   diced
1 green bell pepper, seeded and
   diced
1 serrano or Thai chile, seeded
   and minced
1 tablespoon water
3 tablespoons fermented black
   beans
1 tablespoon dry sherry
1 tablespoon oyster sauce
⅔ cup beef stock (page 186)
1 tablespoon cornstarch
½ teaspoon sugar

2 scallions, finely sliced on a
   diagonal, for garnish

Although beef in Chinese cuisine is usually sliced or cubed and then cooked, this recipe provides a delicious exception by offering a traditional black bean sauce to accompany filet steaks. The tangy salted and fermented black beans are made with soy beans, and because they are affordable and easy to prepare, they have always been favored in China as a condiment and seasoning ingredient. The sauce also contains the Cantonese dark brown oyster sauce, a concentrated all-purpose seasoning and table condiment made with oysters that have been stewed down with soy sauce, salt or brine, and cornstarch. Both fermented black beans and oyster sauce are available in jars in the Asian food section of your supermarket or at any Asian market. Serve this dish with stir-fried vegetables (page 164) if you wish.

••

To prepare the steaks, mix together the soy sauce and chile oil in a cup and rub all over the steaks. Let the steaks sit on a plate at room temperature for 15 minutes before cooking.

Meanwhile, prepare the rice.

Heat a heavy sauté pan or skillet and sear the steaks for 4 to 5 minutes per side for medium-rare or 6 to 7 minutes per side for medium.

While the steaks are cooking, prepare the sauce. Heat the oil in a separate pan or skillet and add the garlic, ginger, bell peppers, and chile, and sauté over high heat for 1 minute. Add the water, being careful not to let it splash, and let the vegetables steam for 1 minute. Add the black beans, sherry, and oyster sauce, and stir well. Thoroughly mix the stock, cornstarch, and sugar in a cup, raise the heat to high, and add to the pan. Bring to a boil, lower the heat to medium-high, and stir to combine for 1 minute, until the sauce has thickened. Remove from the heat.

To serve, place the steaks on warm serving plates and spoon the rice next to the filets. Ladle the black bean sauce over the steaks, garnish with the scallions, and serve immediately.

Indonesian Satay Beef Kebabs with Jasmine Rice

SERVES 4

For the Beef:
2 pounds top sirloin steak, cut
    into ¼- to ⅓-inch-thick strips

For the Marinade:
3 garlic cloves, sliced
½ onion, chopped
1 tablespoon chopped fresh
    cilantro leaves
1 tablespoon brown sugar
Juice of 1 lime (about
    2 tablespoons)
1 tablespoon Asian fish sauce
1 tablespoon olive oil

For the Rice:
2 cups jasmine rice

For the Peanut Sauce:
2 cups canned coconut milk
1 stalk fresh lemongrass, thinly
    sliced (optional)
½ cup peanut butter
1 onion, minced
1 tablespoon brown sugar
1 teaspoon pure red chile
    powder or cayenne
1 tablespoon Asian fish sauce
1 tablespoon soy sauce
¼ cup toasted shaved coconut,
    for garnish (optional)

Satay is a classic Indonesian dish. Marinated strips or cubes of meat or fish are skewered and cooked, then typically served with a spicy peanut sauce, which is the style we have chosen here. Metal or wooden skewers may be used for this recipe; if wooden, soak them first in water for an hour or so to prevent them from burning up on the grill. The long-grained jasmine rice is wonderfully aromatic and a traditional style of rice in Thailand and other parts of southeast Asia. Many large supermarkets carry it in their Asian food sections, or it may be purchased in Asian grocery stores. (The same is true of the fermented fish sauce called for in this recipe.)

• •

Thread the meat on 20 wooden skewers (or 10 large metal skewers), place in a deep dish, and set aside.

Combine all the marinade ingredients in a food processor or blender and puree until smooth. Pour the marinade over the skewered meat, cover, and let sit for 1 hour at room temperature.

Preheat the grill (or, alternatively, the kebabs can be broiled).

Thoroughly rinse the rice under cold running water until the water runs clear. Drain the rice and transfer to a saucepan. Cover with 2½ cups of water and bring to a boil. Lower the heat to a simmer, cover the pan, and cook for 5 to 10 minutes, until the water is absorbed and the rice is just cooked and firm in texture. Cover the pan to keep warm.

While the rice is cooking, prepare the sauce. Combine the coconut milk and lemongrass in a saucepan and bring to a boil. Lower the heat and simmer for 10 minutes. Remove the pan from the heat and strain through a fine-mesh sieve into a clean saucepan. Stir in the remaining ingredients and bring to a boil. Turn the heat to the lowest setting and keep warm.

Remove the skewers from the marinade. Place on the grill (or under the broiler) and cook for 2 to 3 minutes, turning often.

To serve, spoon the rice onto the middle of each serving plate. Arrange the skewers on each serving of rice and drizzle with the peanut sauce. Garnish with the shaved coconut if desired and serve immediately.

Filet Mignon Steaks with Sichuan Peppercorn Sauce

By Chef Susanna Foo, Susanna Foo Chinese Cuisine, Philadelphia, Pennsylvania

SERVES 6

For the Sichuan Peppercorn Oil:
2 tablespoons Sichuan
    peppercorns
1 cup corn or olive oil
3 garlic cloves

For the Steaks and Marinade:
2 tablespoons brandy
1½ pounds filet mignon steaks,
    trimmed well and cut into
    ½-inch-thick slices
1 tablespoon cornstarch
1 tablespoon corn oil

For the Rice:
2 cups medium-grain rice

For the Stir-Fry:
½ cup corn oil
¼ cup chopped onion
2 garlic cloves, minced
1 teaspoon minced ginger
1 teaspoon dried green
    peppercorns
½ cup beef stock (page 186)
1 teaspoon cornstarch
1 tablespoon soy sauce
1 teaspoon kosher salt
1 red bell pepper, seeded and
    julienned
¼ cup chopped fresh cilantro
    leaves

Mountainous Sichuan in western China is the largest of all the country's provinces. The cuisine is renowned for its assertive flavors and fieriness, due largely to the abundant use of chiles and the small, brown, aromatic Sichuan peppercorns. Susanna tells us, "Sichuan peppercorns are as important in Chinese cookery as black peppercorns are in the Western world. Even though they originated in the Sichuan province, they are widely used all over China." Beef is consumed more in Sichuan than in many other parts of China, and it is invariably cut into bite-size pieces and stir-fried as in this recipe.

••

To prepare the peppercorn oil, toast the peppercorns in a hot, dry skillet. Turn the heat to medium-low and shake the skillet or stir frequently, for 15 to 20 minutes, or until the peppercorns are dark brown and fragrant. Heat the oil in a saucepan until very hot. Add the peppercorns and garlic, and cook for 2 minutes over high heat. Turn off the heat and let cool. Pour into an airtight bottle or container and store in a cool, dry place. The remainder of the oil not used in this recipe will keep for three months if stored properly.

To prepare the steaks, place the brandy and filets in a mixing bowl, add the cornstarch, and toss together to coat. Add the oil and mix well, making sure the pieces of meat are separated from one another. Cover the bowl with plastic wrap and marinate in the refrigerator for 1 hour.

Wash the rice 2 or 3 times until the water is clear, and drain well. Place 2 cups of water in a heavy saucepan with a tight-fitting lid and bring to a boil over high heat. Add the rice, turn the heat to very low, and stir once to loosen any grains sticking to the bottom. Cook for 5 minutes and then cover the pan. Simmer the rice for 15 minutes, without lifting the lid. Remove the pan from the heat and let stand, covered, for 10 minutes, or until all the water is absorbed. Fluff with a fork just before serving.

To prepare the stir-fry, heat the oil in a wok to 350 degrees. Add the beef in 2 batches, using a fork or chopsticks to separate the pieces as they cook. Cook for about 2 minutes, or until the steak is seared and well done outside but rare inside. Remove the steak from the wok with a slotted spoon, drain on paper towels, and keep warm. Strain off the oil and reserve for another use.

Heat 2 tablespoons of the peppercorn oil in a clean wok or skillet. Add the onion, garlic, ginger, and peppercorns, and stir-fry over high heat for 1 to 2 minutes, or until the onion is golden. Mix the stock with the cornstarch in a cup and add to the wok. Add the soy sauce, salt, and bell pepper, and stir-fry for 2 minutes or until heated through. Return the steak to the wok, add the cilantro, and stir-fry until the sauce thoroughly coats the meat, about 3 minutes.

Transfer the rice and stir-fry to separate serving bowls and let your guests serve themselves.

Susanna Foo was born in Inner Mongolia, China, and raised in Taipei. She came to the United States in 1967 to earn an advanced degree in library science. In 1979 Susanna and her husband moved to Philadelphia to join his family's restaurant business, and there she discovered her vocation. Cooking has always been a family affair; she learned Hunan-style cooking from her mother-in-law and Chinese northern-style pasta from her cousin. The founder of the Culinary Institute of America, the late Jacob Rosenthal, encouraged Susanna to take a course at the institute, and following this she and her husband opened their own restaurant, Susanna Foo Chinese Cuisine, in downtown Philadelphia in 1987. Susanna reinterprets classical Chinese dishes using French techniques, fresh ingredients, and herbs, spices, and seasonings from around the world. In 1995 her first cookbook, *Susanna Foo Chinese Cuisine,* was published by Chapters and received the James Beard Foundation Award for Best International Cookbook.

Canton Beef with Stir-Fried Vegetables and Mango

For the Marinade:
2 tablespoons soy sauce
2 tablespoons water
1 teaspoon cornstarch
1 teaspoon hot chile oil
1 teaspoon minced garlic

For the Beef:
1 pound top sirloin steak, about
    1 inch thick, cut into ½-inch
    strips about 2 to 3 inches long

For the Rice:
2 cups long-grain rice
1 tablespoon scallions finely
    sliced on a diagonal

For the Stir-Fry:
4 Chinese dried mushrooms or
    8 fresh shiitakes, stemmed
    and sliced
4 tablespoons (¼ cup) peanut oil
1 red bell pepper, seeded and
    julienned
1 carrot, cut in half lengthwise
    and sliced on a diagonal
¼ cup bamboo shoots, drained
    and julienned
2 scallions, sliced on a diagonal
2 tablespoons water
1 mango, peeled, pitted, and
    julienned

The southern Chinese province of Canton enjoys a semitropical climate and a long coastline so that high-quality produce, seafood, and livestock are in abundant supply. The province has long been renowned for its refined and flavorful cuisine. Because a high proportion of the first Chinese immigrants to the United States and Europe came from the Canton province in the nineteenth century, this particular regional style of cooking is probably the best known in the West and synonymous with "Chinese cooking." The technique of stir-frying, which preserves color, texture, and nutritional values, is typical of the cuisine. Meat is often marinated and also frequently accompanied by fruit as in this recipe.

....

To prepare the marinade, combine all the ingredients in a mixing bowl. Add the sliced steak and let sit at room temperature for 1 hour or refrigerate overnight.

Place the rice in a strainer under cold running water until the water no longer looks milky. Transfer the rice to a saucepan with 2 cups of water and bring to a boil. Stir once to prevent the rice from sticking to the bottom of the pan. Turn the heat to low, cover the pan, and cook for 15 minutes, or until the liquid is absorbed. Turn off the heat and let the rice stand for 10 minutes. Keep warm. Fluff with a fork just before serving and garnish with the scallions.

To prepare the stir-fry, rehydrate the mushrooms by soaking them in warm water for 15 minutes. Drain and squeeze gently to remove the excess moisture. Remove the stalks and dice.

Heat 2 tablespoons of the oil in a wok or deep skillet. Remove the beef from the marinade and pat dry. Quickly stir-fry the beef in 2 or 3 batches over high heat for 1 to 2 minutes, until well browned on all sides but rare or medium-rare inside. Remove the beef and keep warm. Wipe out the wok with a paper towel and heat the remaining 2 tablespoons of oil. Add the diced mushrooms, bell

pepper, carrot, bamboo shoots, and scallions, and stir-fry for a few seconds over high heat. Carefully add the water to steam the vegetables and stir until it has evaporated. Add the mango and reserved beef, warm through, and remove from the heat.

To serve, spoon a bed of the rice onto warm serving plates and top with the stir-fry. Serve immediately.

9

Steak Recipes from Central and South America

Cuban Breaded Steaks with Red Beans and Rice

SERVES 4

For the Red Beans and Rice:
1 cup dried pinto beans, rinsed
    and soaked overnight
2 ounces smoked bacon (or
    2 large slices), diced
2 ounces lean ham, diced
1 tablespoon light olive oil
2 garlic cloves, minced
½ onion, diced
½ small green bell pepper,
    seeded and diced
¼ teaspoon ground cumin
⅛ teaspoon dried oregano
¼ teaspoon freshly ground black
    pepper
½ teaspoon salt, or to taste
1 cup long-grain white rice

For the Marinade:
3 cloves garlic, minced to a
    paste
¼ teaspoon salt
¼ teaspoon freshly ground black
    pepper
⅛ teaspoon cayenne
2 tablespoons freshly squeezed
    lemon juice
½ cup freshly squeezed lime
    juice

Christopher Columbus described Cuba as "the most beautiful land that human eyes have ever seen," and the country has a distinctive and sophisticated cuisine. It is unfortunate for all food lovers (among others) that Cuba has been isolated from the United States since the revolution in 1959 that brought Fidel Castro to power. However, a stroll or drive along Calle Ocho (Eighth Street) in Miami's Little Havana district will give you a good sense of the character of the cuisine as you take in the sights, sounds, and aromas of the food markets and restaurants. Beef features prominently in Cuban cuisine, and cattle raising is an important part of the country's agriculture. This recipe, called Bistec Empanizado in Cuba, is a classic preparation; a similar version (but without the breading) that is equally popular in Cuban homes and on menus in Miami and Havana alike is called Bistec de Palomilla. Red beans and rice is a classic Cuban side dish called Congrí.

· ·

To prepare the red beans and rice, drain and rinse the soaked beans and place in a saucepan with enough fresh cold water to cover by 2 to 3 inches. Slowly bring to a simmer and cook at a low simmer until just tender, about 1½ to 2 hours, adding more water as necessary to keep the beans covered. Drain the beans, reserving 4 cups of the cooking liquid.

In a large, dry, heavy skillet, sauté the bacon over medium heat for about 5 minutes, until crisp. Remove and drain on paper towels. Add the ham to the skillet and sauté in the rendered bacon fat, stirring occasionally, for about 5 minutes, until lightly browned. Remove the ham and drain on paper towels. Add the oil to the skillet and sauté the garlic, onion, and bell pepper over medium-high heat for 3 to 4 minutes, stirring occasionally. Add the 4 cups of reserved cooking liquid from the beans, the reserved cooked bacon and ham, the cumin, oregano, pepper, salt, and rice. Bring the mixture to a boil, turn the heat to low, and cover the pan. Simmer for about 20 minutes. Uncover the pan, stir in the reserved beans, and simmer for 5 to 10 minutes, until the liquid has been absorbed.

While the rice is cooking, thoroughly combine all the marinade ingredients in a large shallow dish. Gently pound out the steaks with a flat-sided meat mallet to a thickness of ¼ inch. Add to the dish and marinate at room temperature for 20 minutes, turning occasionally.

Remove the steaks from the marinade and pat dry. Place the eggs in a shallow bowl and mix the bread crumbs with the parsley on a plate. Dredge the steaks first in the egg wash and then in the bread crumbs, coating them well. Heat 2 tablespoons of the oil in a heavy sauté pan or skillet and sauté 2 steaks at a time over medium-high heat for about 2 minutes per side for medium rare or 3 to 4 minutes per side for medium, and the bread crumb coating is golden brown. Repeat for the remaining steaks.

To serve, place the steaks on warm serving plates and garnish with a small mound of onion topped with the parsley. Spoon the red beans and rice to the side of the steaks and serve immediately.

For the Steaks:
4 top sirloin steaks, about
   6 ounces each

For the Breading:
3 eggs, beaten
1 cup fine bread crumbs
1 tablespoon minced fresh
   flat-leaf parsley

4 tablespoons (¼ cup) light olive
   oil
3 tablespoons minced white
   onion, for garnish
3 tablespoons minced fresh
   flat-leaf parsley, for garnish

Caribbean Creole Steaks with Cinnamon Rice

SERVES 4

For the Marinade:
3 tablespoons olive oil
2 tablespoons red wine vinegar
5 tablespoons dark rum
2 cloves garlic, minced to a
*   paste*
Salt
Freshly ground black pepper

For the Steaks:
4 boneless rib-eye steaks, about
*   8 ounces each*

For the Cinnamon Rice:
1 cup white long-grain rice
2 tablespoons butter
½ white onion, finely diced
1 carrot, finely diced
½ stalk celery, finely diced
¼ teaspoon salt
2 teaspoons ground cinnamon
3 tablespoons raisins

Creole cuisine, most closely associated in the United States with Louisiana, describes a spicy, sophisticated style of cooking that combines French, Spanish, and African influences and applies equally to the foods of the West Indies and parts of South America and the Gulf Coast of North America. The term "creole" is used in French-speaking areas while "criolla" is the Spanish-speaking equivalent. This dish is our adaptation of a traditional dish from the French West Indies, and the sauce contains tomatoes, bell peppers, and celery, ingredients that are hallmarks of Creole cooking. The hint of sweetness in the cinnamon rice provides the perfect foil for the picante sauce.

• •

To prepare the marinade, combine all the ingredients in a large dish. Add the steaks and marinate at room temperature for 2 hours, turning occasionally.

Prepare the grill. (Or, alternatively, the steaks can be broiled or sautéed in a heavy pan or skillet using 1 tablespoon of hot olive oil or safflower oil; they will take approximately the same time to cook as they will on the grill.)

To prepare the rice, rinse it in a strainer under cold running water until the water no longer looks milky. Drain and set aside. Heat 1 tablespoon of the butter in a saucepan and sauté the onion, carrot, and celery over low heat for 8 minutes, stirring occasionally. Add the rice, salt, cinnamon, raisins, and 2½ cups of water, and bring to a boil over high heat. When the water is reduced to the level of the rice, turn the heat to low and cover the pan. Simmer for about 15 minutes, or until the water is absorbed, stirring occasionally. Remove the pan from the heat and let stand

For the Creole Sauce:
2 tablespoons olive oil
2 cloves garlic, minced
1 onion, diced
½ red bell pepper, seeded and
  diced
½ green bell pepper, seeded and
  diced
½ green or orange habanero
  chile, seeded and finely
  minced, or 1 serrano chile,
  seeded and minced
1 small stalk celery, diced
1 scallion, finely sliced
1 tablespoon minced fresh
  oregano
½ teaspoon ground cumin
2 ripe tomatoes, seeded and
  diced
¼ cup red wine
2 tablespoons red wine vinegar
½ cup beef stock (page 186)
Salt
Freshly ground black pepper

for 5 minutes. Add the remaining tablespoon of butter and fluff with a fork just before serving.

To prepare the sauce, heat the oil in a heavy sauté pan or skillet and add the garlic, onion, bell peppers, chile, celery, and scallion, and sauté over medium-high heat for 1 minute. Stir in the oregano, cumin, and tomatoes, and sauté 1 minute longer. Add the wine, vinegar, and stock, and bring to a boil. Lower the heat, season with salt and pepper, and simmer for 5 minutes. Keep warm.

While the sauce is simmering, prepare the steaks. Remove the steaks from the marinade and pat dry; reserve the marinade. Grill the steaks for 4 to 5 minutes per side for medium-rare or about 6 minutes for medium, basting with the marinade while the steaks are grilling.

To serve, spoon a bed of rice onto warm serving plates and place the steaks on top of the rice. Ladle the sauce next to the steaks and serve immediately.

Carne Rellena with Fried Plantains

For the Carne Rellena:
2 pounds flank steak
3 cloves garlic, crushed or
    minced to a paste
1 teaspoon salt
¼ teaspoon freshly ground black
    pepper
½ teaspoon dried oregano
4 ounces ham, thinly sliced
½ onion, sliced
1 carrot, thinly sliced
1 red Fresno or jalapeño chile,
    seeded and minced
1 red bell pepper, seeded and
    julienned
2 hard-boiled eggs, sliced
3 tablespoons light olive or
    safflower oil
¼ cup tomato paste
1 tablespoon Worcestershire
    sauce
1 tablespoon red wine vinegar
1½ cups beef stock (page 186)
1 cup red wine
2 bay leaves

For the Fried Plantains:
Peanut oil
2 ripe plantains, peeled and cut
    on a diagonal into ⅓-inch
    slices
Freshly ground black pepper

Stuffing steak is a common technique in many parts of Central and South America, and this dish is known as matambre in some countries—a contraction meaning "kill hunger" from the Spanish words "matar" (to kill) and "hambre" (hunger). There are endless variations on the theme—in Venezuela, for example, the eggs are sometimes cooked as an omelet rather than hard-boiling them before they are added as a layer of stuffing. If you prefer this option, by all means try it. You can also add some sliced mushrooms or substitute the vegetables of your choice. Fried plantains are typical of the Caribbean and tropical regions of Central America where they are used as a starch. Plantains are members of the banana family and are sometimes marketed as "cooking bananas." Use only really ripe plantains that have a completely black skin. If they are hard to find in your region, substitute plain rice (page 162) or black beans (page 188).

• •

Preheat the oven to 350 degrees.

Lay the beef on a flat work surface and spread the top side with the garlic paste. Season with the salt, pepper, and oregano. Add layers of the ham, onion, carrot, chile, and bell pepper. Add the eggs last. Each ingredient should be arranged so that it fits at least a ½ inch inside the edge of the steak. Carefully roll the steak up like a jelly roll and tie at each end and in the middle with kitchen twine.

Heat the olive oil in a heavy sauté pan or skillet and sear the stuffed steak over medium-high heat about 2 to 3 minutes on each side, until brown on all sides. Place the steak in a roasting pan. Mix together the tomato paste, Worcestershire sauce, vinegar, stock, wine, and bay leaves in a mixing bowl and pour into the roasting pan.

Transfer the roasting pan to the oven and cook, turning occasionally, for about 2 hours, or until the steak is tender.

Meanwhile, to prepare the fried plantains, heat ½ inch of oil in a deep, heavy skillet to 375 degrees. Carefully add the plantain slices and fry for 2 to 3 minutes per side, until golden brown. Drain on paper towels, season with pepper, and keep warm.

To serve, remove the steak from the oven and place on a cutting board. Let rest for 5 minutes before carefully carving into slices. Meanwhile, pour the braising liquid into a saucepan and reduce over high heat until thickened. Place the sliced stuffed steak on warm serving plates and ladle the sauce over. Serve with the fried plantains.

Chili Con Carne

1 pound top sirloin steak, diced
Salt
Freshly ground black pepper
3 tablespoons light olive oil
2 cloves garlic, minced
1 white onion, diced
3 tablespoons ancho or pure red
    chile powder
½ teaspoon ground cumin
1 tablespoon all-purpose flour
1 cup tomato paste
1¼ cups beef stock (page 186)
1 cup cooked black beans
    (page 188)
8 flour tortillas
1 cup grated smoked cheese, for
    garnish (optional)
¼ cup sliced scallions, for
    garnish (optional)

The foods of northern Mexico and especially the cuisines of Sonora and Chihuahua have long provided inspiration for Texas and southwestern cooking so that today they have a great deal in common. Cattle were raised on ranches in northern Mexico long before they were introduced across the border, and vaqueros—the Mexican cowboys—no doubt made campfire stews similar to this before their North American counterparts popularized the ubiquitous "bowl of red." Chili con carne was probably adapted originally from Caldillos or Cazuelas, beef stews that were unusual in that they were cooked by men rather than women. Great pride was taken in achieving the hottest and tastiest chile. Literally "chile with meat," chili con carne may or may not contain beans; versions in northern Mexico often do, while those north of the border (and especially in Texas) usually do not.

· ·

To prepare the chili con carne, season the diced steak with salt and pepper. Heat the oil in a heavy-bottomed saucepan and sear the steak over high heat, while stirring, for about 2 minutes, or until brown on all sides. Remove the meat and set aside. Add a little more oil if necessary, then add the garlic and onion, and sauté for 2 minutes, until soft and light golden. Lower the heat to medium and add the chile powder, cumin, and flour, and mix well. Return the meat to the pan and coat thoroughly. Add the tomato paste and 1 cup of the stock, and bring to a boil. Turn the heat to low and simmer for 30 minutes, stirring occasionally. Add the remaining ¼ cup of stock, the beans, and a little water if necessary. Adjust the seasonings and stir the chili well to distribute all the ingredients evenly.

To serve, warm the tortillas in a dry skillet or for 3 to 4 minutes in an oven heated to 250 degrees. Spoon the chili into warm serving bowls and sprinkle with the cheese and scallions if desired. Serve with the warm tortillas.

Argentinean Churrasco con Chimichurri and Sweet Potato Fries

By Chef Douglas Rodriguez, Patria, New York, New York

SERVES 4

For the Chimichurri:
¼ cup red wine vinegar
6 garlic cloves
3 bay leaves
2 jalapeño chiles, seeded and
*   coarsely chopped*
1½ tablespoons salt
¾ cup coarsely chopped fresh
*   parsley*
¼ cup fresh oregano leaves
⅓ cup extra-virgin olive oil

For the Sweet Potato Fries:
3 large sweet potatoes
2 to 3 cups canola oil
Salt

For the Steaks:
3 filet mignon steaks,
*   7 to 8 ounces each*
Salt
Freshly ground pepper

Here's a dish that takes us down to South America and the Argentinean pampas, home of the gauchos, the continent's cowboys. Chimichurri is a traditional condiment that's similar to a pesto sauce but made with parsley rather than basil. It's the typical accompaniment for the classic Argentinean dish, churrasco, which is usually made with skirt steak. In this recipe, Doug uses filet mignon, which is the preferred cut of the family of Doug's maître d' at Patria, Ariel Lacayo, who owns the famous Los Ranchos steak house in Managua, Nicaragua.

· ·

To prepare the chimichurri, place the vinegar, garlic, bay leaves, jalapeños, and salt in a food processor and blend until smooth. Add the parsley and oregano, and pulse until well blended. Transfer the mixture to a mixing bowl and whisk in the oil. Cover tightly and set aside.

Preheat the oven to 400 degrees and prepare the grill (or, alternatively, the steaks can be broiled).

To prepare the fries, place the sweet potatoes on a baking sheet, bake in the oven for 20 minutes, and let cool. Neatly cut the potatoes, still with their skins on, into thin sticks. Heat the oil in a deep fryer or large saucepan to 350 degrees and fry the potatoes for 3 to 4 minutes, or until golden brown. Remove with a slotted spoon and drain on paper towels. Season with salt and keep warm.

To prepare the steaks, lay a filet on its side on a flat work surface. Using a sharp smooth-edged (not serrated) knife, make a downward cut in the side of the steak of about ¼ inch or slightly less. While rolling the steak to the left, angle the knife so that you are cutting a long, continuous strip of meat (this technique is like "unrolling" a strip from the filet). Repeat for the remaining filets.

Sprinkle the strips of filet with salt and pepper, and place on the hot grill. Grill the strips for about 3 minutes per side for medium or to the desired doneness.

To serve, remove the meat from the grill and place on warm serving plates. Pour the chimichurri over the filets and serve immediately with the sweet potato fries.

Douglas Rodriguez, the son of Cuban immigrants, was raised in Miami and grew up with the sights, smells, and flavors of Cuban-American cuisine. His travels and palate instilled a passion for the cuisines of Latin America, resulting in a fusion cuisine that Doug has named "Nuevo Latino." As early as the age of fourteen, Doug was working as a summer apprentice at the Four Ambassadors Hotel in Miami. He trained professionally at Johnson & Wales University and returned to Florida where he became the chef at the Wet Paint Cafe in Miami Beach. Then in 1989, Doug opened Yuca, an upscale Cuban-style restaurant in Coral Gables where he drew national attention. In 1994 he moved to New York to open the highly acclaimed Patria, where his Nuevo Latino cuisine is showcased. Among numerous other awards, Doug was nominated for the Rising Star Chef of the Year by the James Beard Foundation in 1991, 1993, and 1995, and won the award in 1996. His first cookbook, *Nuevo Latino,* was published by Ten Speed Press in 1995.

Ranchero Steaks with Refried Black Beans

For the Steaks:
⅛ teaspoon salt
⅛ teaspoon ground cumin
⅛ teaspoon ground coriander
4 tablespoons (¼ cup) light olive
    oil
4 boneless rib-eye steaks, about
    10 ounces each

For the Refried Beans:
2 tablespoons vegetable oil
1 teaspoon minced garlic
2 tablespoons minced white
    onion
2 cups cooked black beans
    (page 188)
¼ teaspoon salt
1 tablespoon minced fresh
    cilantro
3 tablespoons crumbled goat
    cheese (optional)

For the Ranchero Sauce:
1 pound Roma (plum) tomatoes
2 serrano chiles or 1 jalapeño
    chile
1 tablespoon light olive oil
1 teaspoon minced garlic
½ cup finely diced white onion
2 poblano chiles or 3 green New
    Mexico or Anaheim chiles,
    roasted, peeled, seeded, and
    finely diced (page 189)
¼ teaspoon salt
2 tablespoons chopped fresh
    cilantro

This steak dish, prepared in the rustic Mexican style, features a staple tomato sauce that is typically made early in the morning in restaurants and market food stands all across the country. It is then used with all kinds of dishes, from corn to fish and beef, throughout the day. Probably the best-known recipe that incorporates this sauce is Huevos Rancheros, which provides another example of its versatility. Of course, tomatoes are native to the New World, so although most people think of Italy when they taste a rich tomato-based sauce, the original versions were enjoyed hundreds of years earlier in Central and South America.

Refried beans are another favorite food found across Mexico; in the north, they tend to be made with red pinto beans, while in the south, refried black beans are more common. The secret to great refried beans is that there be enough oil in the pan to keep them moist on the bottom while they develop a thin, smooth crust on top.

••

Combine the salt, cumin, coriander, and oil in a shallow dish or bowl. Massage the steaks with this mixture and let sit at room temperature for 1 hour.

Meanwhile, prepare the beans. Heat the oil in a heavy, deep-sided skillet or nonstick pan and sauté the garlic and onion over medium heat for about 5 minutes, until tender. Mash or roughly puree the beans and mix with the salt and cilantro in a mixing bowl before adding to the pan. Turn the heat to medium-low and cook the beans for about 10 minutes, using a spatula to prevent them from sticking to the bottom of the pan. The beans should look dry and a little crusty on top. Keep warm and sprinkle the goat cheese over just before serving if desired.

Prepare the grill and preheat the broiler. (The steaks can also be broiled rather than grilled if you prefer.)

To prepare the sauce, place the tomatoes and serrano chiles under the broiler and sear, turning often, about 5 minutes, until lightly blackened on all sides. Remove, chop together, and set aside. Heat the oil in a heavy sauté pan or skillet and sauté the garlic and onion over medium-low heat for 6 or 7 minutes, until soft but not brown. Add the blackened tomatoes and serrano chiles, the roasted poblano chiles, and salt. Turn the heat to low, cover the pan, and simmer for about 20 minutes, adding a little water if necessary. Stir in the cilantro just before serving.

While the sauce is cooking, grill the steaks for about 5 minutes per side for medium-rare or 6 to 7 minutes per side for medium. To serve, place the steaks on warm serving plates and ladle the sauce over the steaks. Spoon the beans to the side of the steaks and serve immediately.

Garlic-Stuffed Pampas Steaks with Red Chile Sauce and Latin Lentils

For the Red Chile Sauce:
4 ounces dried guajillo chiles or
    dried red New Mexico or
    Anaheim chiles
5 Roma (plum) tomatoes
½ teaspoon ground cumin
½ teaspoon ground dried
    oregano
2 tablespoons light olive oil
2 garlic cloves, minced
½ onion, diced
½ teaspoon salt

For the Latin Lentils:
1 cup green lentils, picked
    through and rinsed
2 tablespoons light olive oil
2 garlic cloves, minced
1 onion, diced
4 Roma (plum) tomatoes,
    seeded and diced
Salt
Freshly ground black pepper
½ tablespoon minced fresh
    cilantro

For the Steaks:
4 boneless rib-eye steaks, about
    10 ounces each
12 garlic cloves, cut in half
    lengthwise
Salt
Freshly ground black pepper
2 tablespoons light olive oil

If you are a true steak and garlic lover and enjoy the smooth, complex flavors of a picante chile sauce, then this is definitely the dish for you. If you are particularly bold, you might want to try stuffing slivers of hot red chile into the steaks along with the garlic. To mellow the flavor of the garlic, sauté it in a little oil for 2 to 3 minutes before stuffing the steaks with it.

Lentils are popular in many countries of Latin America, and here they make a robust side dish that stands up well to a hearty, flavorful steak recipe. Occasionally, lentils have a slightly bitter taste, and blanching them before cooking prevents this potential problem.

• •

To prepare the sauce, place the chiles in a single layer in a heavy skillet and dry-roast over medium heat for 2 to 3 minutes, shaking the skillet frequently so they do not burn. Transfer to a mixing bowl and cover with hot water. Let stand for 30 minutes, until the chiles are rehydrated and soft.

Preheat the broiler. Place the tomatoes under the broiler and, turning them often, blacken the skins. Set aside.

Place the cumin and oregano in a small, dry skillet and toast over low heat for about 1 minute, or until fragrant. Set aside.

Heat 1 tablespoon of the oil in a heavy sauté pan or skillet and sauté the garlic and onion over medium heat for 7 or

8 minutes, until just browned. Transfer to a food processor or blender and add the blackened tomatoes, toasted cumin and oregano, salt, rehydrated chiles, and ½ cup of the water in which the chiles rehydrated. (Taste the water; if it is bitter, use ½ cup of fresh water instead.) Puree until smooth, adding a little more water if necessary. Just before you are ready to serve, heat the remaining tablespoon of oil in a clean, deep, heavy skillet; when very hot, add the chile puree. Cook over high heat for 3 or 4 minutes, stirring continuously; add a little more water if necessary to prevent the sauce from becoming too thick.

To prepare the lentils, bring a large saucepan of water to a boil, add the lentils, and blanch for 2 to 3 minutes. Drain the lentils, place them in a clean saucepan, and cover with at least 1 inch of cold water. Bring to a boil, lower the heat, and simmer for 40 to 45 minutes, or until just tender. Drain and set aside.

Heat the oil in a large, heavy sauté pan or skillet and sauté the garlic and onion over medium-high heat for 2 to 3 minutes, until soft. Turn the heat to medium-low, add the tomatoes, salt, and pepper, and sauté for 5 minutes. Stir in the cooked lentils and cilantro, cook 5 minutes longer, and keep warm. Add a little water if necessary.

To prepare the steaks, use a paring knife to make 6 horizontal slits in the side of each steak (3 slits per side). Stuff the slices of garlic in these slits and season the steaks with salt and pepper. Heat the oil in a large, heavy sauté pan or skillet and sear the steaks over medium-high heat for about 4 minutes per side for medium-rare or 5 to 6 minutes per side for medium.

To serve, ladle the sauce on warm serving plates and place the steaks on the sauce. Spoon the lentils next to the steaks and serve immediately.

Carne Asada con Papas y Salsa Roja

SERVES 4

For the Salsa Roja:
2 jalapeño chiles
4 Roma (plum) tomatoes
1 small white onion, stem end
    untrimmed and cut into
    quarters
2 garlic cloves
⅛ teaspoon ground cumin
2 tablespoons chopped fresh
    cilantro
1 tablespoon freshly squeezed
    lime juice
½ teaspoon sugar
Salt

For the Marinade:
8 garlic cloves, crushed or
    minced to a paste
¼ teaspoon ground cumin
¼ teaspoon pure red chile
    powder
¼ teaspoon salt

For the Steaks:
4 top sirloin steaks, about
    10 ounces each

For the Papas:
8 new potatoes
3 tablespoons light olive oil
1 tablespoon finely sliced fresh
    chives
Salt
Freshly ground black pepper

L iterally "grilled meat with potatoes and red salsa," this is a simple, hearty dish containing rustic flavors of flame-blackened tomatoes and chiles, and grilled potatoes and steak. In Mexico, carne asada is most closely associated with a famous and popular combination plate, Carne Asada à la Tampiqueña, that typifies the cuisine of the port city of Tampico and the state of Tamaulipas on Mexico's Gulf Coast. This dish was created in the 1940s—not in Tamaulipas, as one might expect, but by a well-known Mexico City restaurateur, José Inéz Loredo, who hailed from Tampico and wanted to feature a representative plate from his home region. His version of carne asada is traditionally served with poblano chile strips, enchiladas, grilled cheese, and salsa roja; this version is simplified but no less delicious.

••

Preheat the broiler.

To prepare the salsa, place the chiles and tomatoes under the broiler and, turning them often, blacken the skins. Stem and seed the chiles, coarsely chop them together with the tomatoes, and transfer to a mixing bowl.

Heat a sauté pan or skillet over medium-high heat. Add the onion to the pan and dry-roast for 10 minutes, turning often. Add the garlic and dry-roast 10 minutes longer. Remove the onion and garlic from the pan, let cool, and then coarsely chop. Add to the mixing bowl together with the cumin, cilantro, lime juice, sugar, and salt, and mix together. Set aside at room temperature. (If not using within 1 hour, refrigerate and bring to room temperature before using.)

For the marinade, thoroughly combine all the ingredients in a mixing bowl. Rub the mixture on both sides of the steaks and let sit at room temperature for 30 minutes.

Prepare the grill (or, alternatively, the steaks can be broiled).

To prepare the papas, place the potatoes in a saucepan and cover with water. Bring to a boil and cook for 10 minutes. Drain and transfer the potatoes to a bowl of ice water until they are completely cool. Drain the potatoes again, dry thoroughly, and cut into quarters. Place the potatoes in a mixing bowl and toss with the oil, chives, salt, and pepper. Place the potatoes on the hot grill and cook for about 10 minutes, or until light brown and crisp. Keep warm.

Grill the steaks for 4 to 5 minutes per side for medium-rare or about 6 minutes per side for medium; the marinade will give the exterior of the steaks a little crispness.

To serve, place the steaks in the center of each warm serving plate and spoon the salsa next to the steaks. Place the potatoes next to the steaks and salsa.

10

Basic Recipes
and Techniques

Beef Stock

(Chef Bradley Ogden, One Market Restaurant, San Francisco, California)

YIELD: ABOUT 2 QUARTS

2 pounds beef bones, meat, and
   trimmings
2 large carrots, coarsely
   chopped
1 large onion, coarsely chopped
1 leek, coarsely chopped
1 celery stalk, coarsely chopped
2 medium tomatoes, quartered,
   or 1 cup canned plum
   tomatoes
2 garlic cloves, crushed
6 sprigs fresh parsley
1 bay leaf
4 sprigs fresh thyme or
   ½ teaspoon dried thyme
3 tablespoons white wine
   vinegar

Preheat the oven to 450 degrees.

Place the beef bones, meat, and trimmings in a roasting pan with the carrots and onion. Roast in the oven for 30 to 40 minutes, stirring occasionally, until the mixture is browned.

Transfer to a stockpot. Pour off the fat from the roasting pan and deglaze with 2 cups of water, scraping the sides and bottom of the pan to loosen all the pieces. Add this mixture to the stockpot along with the remaining stock ingredients. Add enough water to cover the mixture by 2 inches and bring to a boil. Lower the heat and simmer the stock for at least 4 hours, uncovered. Occasionally skim off any impurities that rise to the top as it cooks. Add more water as necessary to keep the mixture covered. Strain, discard the solids, and let the stock cool. Cover and refrigerate until needed.

Veal Stock

(Chef Roy Yamaguchi, Roy's, Honolulu, Hawaii)

YIELD: ABOUT 2 QUARTS

2 pounds veal bones
¼ cup coarsely chopped celery
¼ cup coarsely chopped carrot
½ cup coarsely chopped onion
*½ cup coarsely chopped
    tomatoes*
*¼ cup coarsely chopped
    mushroom stems*
3 garlic cloves
1 tablespoon tomato puree
½ cup fresh basil leaves
½ teaspoon minced fresh thyme
1 bay leaf, julienned
5 black peppercorns
Salt
Freshly ground black pepper

Preheat the oven to 350 degrees.

Place the veal bones, celery, carrot, onion, tomatoes, mushroom stems, garlic, tomato puree, basil, thyme, bay leaf, and peppercorns in a roasting pan. Mix together well and roast in the oven for 25 to 30 minutes, stirring occasionally, until dark brown.

Transfer to a stockpot. Pour off the fat from the roasting pan and deglaze with a little water, scraping the sides and bottom of the pan to loosen all the pieces. Add this mixture to the stockpot along with enough water to cover the mixture by 2 inches and bring to a boil. Lower the heat and simmer the stock, uncovered, until the liquid is reduced by half. Occasionally skim off any impurities that rise to the top as it cooks. Strain, discard the solids, and let the stock cool. Season with salt and pepper, cover, and refrigerate until needed.

Black Beans

(Chef Mark Miller, Coyote Cafe, Santa Fe, New Mexico)

YIELD: ABOUT 4 CUPS

1 teaspoon ground cumin
1 teaspoon ground coriander
  seeds
1 teaspoon dried ground
  oregano
1 teaspoon dried ground
  marjoram
2 cups dried black beans, picked
  through and rinsed
1 onion, finely diced
3 garlic cloves, minced
2 serrano chiles, seeded and
  minced
2 bay leaves
1 cup tomato puree
1 tablespoon salt
1 cup barbecue sauce, preferably
  smoky-flavored (optional)

You can add the barbecue sauce for spicy southwestern-style beans, but leave it out if you want beans without the smoky flavor.

• •

Place the cumin, coriander, oregano, and marjoram in a dry, heavy skillet and toast over low heat, stirring frequently, for about 1 minute, until fragrant (do not scorch or the mixture will become bitter-tasting). Transfer to a large saucepan and add the beans, onion, garlic, serranos, bay leaves, and tomato puree. Add enough water to cover the beans by 2 to 3 inches. Bring the beans to a simmer over medium heat. Cook at a low simmer for about 2 hours, or until the beans are just tender. Add more water if necessary to keep the beans covered as they cook. Season with salt, stir in the barbecue sauce, and continue cooking the beans for about 10 minutes, or until almost all the liquid is absorbed.

Roasting Garlic

Roasting garlic gives it a sweet, mellow flavor. Place unpeeled garlic cloves in a heavy skillet and dry-roast over low heat for about 30 minutes, shaking or stirring the skillet occasionally, until the garlic becomes soft. Alternatively, place the garlic cloves in a roasting pan and roast in a 350-degree oven for 25 to 30 minutes. (Cooking at 300 degrees for 45 minutes to 1 hour makes the garlic sweeter yet.) When the garlic has roasted, peel the cloves or squeeze them out of the skin.

Roasting Chiles and Bell Peppers

Roasting chiles and bell peppers gives them a complex and attractive smoky flavor. It also makes possible peeling the tough outer skin, which can sometimes be bitter-tasting. Roasting the chiles can be done on the grill, under the broiler, or on a wire rack placed over a gas flame on top of the stove. Blister and blacken the skins evenly, taking care not to burn the flesh. Transfer to a bowl, cover with plastic wrap, and let the chiles "steam" for about 15 minutes. Uncover and remove the charred skins with your fingers or with the tip of a sharp knife. Cut open and remove the seeds and internal ribs—this will help to moderate the heat of the chiles.

Take care to wash your hands thoroughly after handling chiles and never touch your face or eyes with your hands until you have done so. If you have sensitive skin, wear rubber gloves when handling chiles.

Toasting Herbs and Spices

Toasting herbs and spices such as oregano, thyme, and cumin is a technique used especially in southwestern cooking to bring out more complex flavor tones. Place in a dry skillet over low heat and toast, stirring frequently, for about 1 minute, until fragrant. Take care not to scorch herbs or spices, or they will taste bitter.

RESOURCE GUIDE

Steaks and Meat

Omaha Steaks
P.O. Box 3300
Omaha, NE 68103
To order: 1 (800) 228–9055
Customer Service (questions
and inquiries, suggestions):
1 (800) 228–9872

For Information About Meat Nutrition, Food Safety, and Industry Practices

American Meat Institute
Public Affairs Department
P.O. Box 3556
Washington, DC 20007
1 (703) 841–2400

Beef and Veal Culinary Center
National Cattlemen's Beef
Association
444 N. Michigan Avenue
Chicago, IL 60611
1 (312) 467–5520

Kitchen Equipment and Accessories, Including Grills, Smokers, and Tableware

Williams-Sonoma
P.O. Box 7456
San Francisco, CA 94120
1 (800) 541–2233

Grills and Smokers

Barbecues Galore
15041 Bake Parkway
Suite A
Irvine, CA 92618
1 (800) 756–5604

Chef's Catalog
3215 Commercial Ave.
Northbrook, IL 60062
1 (800) 338–3232

Ducane
800 Dutch Square Boulevard
Columbia, SC 29210
1 (803) 798–1600

Charcoal and Smoking Woods

Charcoal Companion
7955 Edgewater Drive
Oakland, CA 94621
1 (800) 521–0505

Lazzari Fuel Co.
P.O. Box 34051
San Francisco, CA 94134
1 (800) 242–7265

Chiles, Hot Sauces, Beans, Seasonings, and Southwestern Ingredients

Coyote Cafe General Store
132 Water Street
Santa Fe, NM 87501
1 (800) 866-HOWL or
(505) 982–2454

Taxco Produce Inc.
1801 S. Good Latimer
Dallas, TX 75226
1 (214) 421–7191

Maytag Blue Cheese and Other Cheeses

Maytag Dairy Farms
P.O. Box 806
Newton, IA 50208
1 (800) 247–2458

INDEX